The Stresses of Work

HEALTH
& SAFETY IN
THE WORKPLACE

The Stresses of Work

McDonald and Doyle

Nelson

Thomas Nelson and Sons Ltd
Nelson House Mayfield Road
Walton-on-Thames Surrey KT12 5PL

PO Box 18123 Nairobi Kenya

116-D JTC Factory Building
Lorong 3 Geylang Square Singapore 1438

Thomas Nelson Australia Pty Ltd
19–39 Jeffcott Street West Melbourne Victoria 3003

Nelson Canada Ltd
81 Curlew Drive Don Mills Ontario M3A 2R1

Thomas Nelson (Hong Kong) Ltd
Watson Estate Block A 13 Floor,
Watson Road Causeway Bay Hong Kong

Thomas Nelson (Nigeria) Ltd
8 Ilupeju Bypass PMB 21303   Ikeja Lagos

Phototypeset in Linotron 202 Univers by
Western Printing Services Ltd, Bristol
Printed in Great Britain by
Ebenezer Baylis & Son Ltd,
The Trinity Press,
Worcester, and London

Contents

Tables and Figures

Tables

Figures

Technical terms

Terms included in the glossary are printed in **bold** the first time they are mentioned in the text.

Preface

Work is a dangerous place. It always has been. It always will be as long as human beings have to operate the processes of production. And even when we have a workforce of white coated, robot ordering button pushers the pressures on the human personality and the lethal potential of the materials of production will still constitute hazards.

None of that is news. Indeed the menace of the workplace is enlarged and increased by the complacency with which so many workers, managers and owners still regard the endemic dangers of work. That is understandable – if people attended work in a mood of constant terror nothing would get done and the psychiatry industry would be the only one offering full employment. But however natural that contemptuous familiarity may seem to be, it is not and never has been, acceptable. Work is not war. There is no unavoidable need for casualties and no justification for succumbing to the idea that disease, disablement and death are tragic but inevitable costs of production.

There are few in any saloon bar, shop floor or boardroom who would disagree with that attitude towards the dangers of work. But putting it into universal practice is a different matter. Legislation, good industrial practice and common sense all help. Vigilance and experience are great protectors. But all of those need the stimulation and re-enforcement of education. This was true when learning caution and safe practices at the workplace was a matter of 'watching Jack'. It is even more crucial when the dangers are subtle, insidious, treacherously corrosive and secretly poisonous.

Now those dangers must be understood and anticipated as well as being treated with respect and avoided. When the materials of work maim and kill people gradually from the inside instead of dramatically from the outside, the responsibility for preventing pain and saving life is on a different scale of complexity and requires a new degree of commitment.

In a perfect world we could expect employers to insist that (as a former Chief Factory Inspector put it) 'the technology of control matches the technology of production' and even in a world that is a long way short of Utopia, many employers do take great and expensive pains to safeguard against the dangers of work. But several factors, from employers' over-confidence in their preventative provision to profit obsession and from callousness to plain ignorance, mean that a great responsibility for the identification and removal of hazards must still be borne by Trade Unions. Their pre-eminent duty is to their members, their perception of all problems must be primarily from the point of view of those members. No other institution has the collective strength or the vested interest to assert that – as my father told me before my first shift in the steelworks – 'prevention is always better than cure, but when there is no cure don't take anything but prevention' and to give practical effect to that maxim.

The Trade Union movement must, therefore, use every opportunity for Health and Safety education and employ its authority to ensure universal understanding of danger among its members, universal expertise and self-confidence among safety representatives and universal resistance to operating any machine or working with any process which can cripple or kill.

This book and its companion volumes on the biological, chemical and physical hazards of work will be important assets for Trade Unionists in general and safety representatives in particular. In the best traditions of the Workers' Educational Association it broadens understanding and knowledge by explaining in clear and practical terms the sources of danger, the extent and nature of danger and the means of identifying and preventing it.

I hope that *The Stresses of Work* will be used as a handbook, a textbook, a work of reference and a source of information. But most of all I hope that it is used for the purpose which the Workers' Educational Association intends – for action in ensuring that knowledge is as much a key to safety as it is a means of power.

Neil Kinnock, M.P.

1 Introduction

This book is about mental and physical health at work, and ways in which psychological and social aspects of working conditions can harm the health and wellbeing of workers. Those aspects of the working environment which cause such problems are known as **stresses**; they result in **strains** and pressures on workers; and prolonged strain can result in serious consequences for health.

The World Health Organisation (WHO) has defined occupational health as:

'The promotion of the highest degree of physical, mental and social wellbeing of workers in all occupations; the prevention among workers of departures from health caused by their working conditions; the protection of workers in their employment from risks resulting from factors adverse to health; the placing and maintenance of the worker in an occupational environment adapted to his/her physiological and psychological condition.'

There are three main implications of this definition:

- Health involves more than being *not ill*; it involves actually feeling *well* and *healthy*. Thus the emphasis is on positive wellbeing as well as on the prevention of disease.
- Health involves not only physical aspects of the functioning of the body, but also having a healthy and satisfying mental and social life.
- The circumstances of work should be organised to promote the wellbeing of workers and should be adapted to meet each worker's needs, skills and aspirations.

If we accept this definition it is clear that a large proportion of workers have jobs which do not promote their health and wellbeing, and that the stresses of work are not just rare situations where people crack up under intolerable strain, but are part and parcel of many people's ordinary working lives. Table 1 summarises some of these stresses together with some of their effects. This shows that there are a huge number of potential stresses at

Table 1 Stresses, strains and their long-term consequences

Stresses	Strains	Long-term consequences
Poverty, insecurity of work and unemployment	*Physical reactions* Headaches, backache, muscle cramps, poor sleep, indigestion	*Physical health* Coronary heart disease, hypertension, gastro-intestinal disorders, poor general health
Excessive overtime, shiftwork	*Psychological reactions* Fatigue, anxiety, tension, irritability, depression, boredom, inability to concentrate, feelings of unreality, low self-esteem	
Pressure of work – excessive pace, mechanical pacing, production deadlines		*Mental health* Poor mental health; chronic anxiety, depression, insomnia, neuroses
Work that is monotonous and requires little skill but demands constant attention		
Working in danger	*Behavioural effects* Heavy indulgence in smoking, alcohol and drugs; impulsive, emotional behaviour; accidents	*Social consequences* Family and marriage disharmony and breakdown; breakdown of social and community relationships
Interpersonal conflicts and tensions		
Uncertain responsibilities		
Social isolation at work	*Social effects* Poor relationships with others at home and at work; inability to fulfil social and family roles; social isolation	
Poor physical environment at work (e.g. noise)		

Note: Factors outside work can also combine with the stresses of work to increase the strain on a worker, e.g. housing problems, domestic and family problems, bereavement, racial prejudice, etc.

work and that virtually every worker is likely to suffer from some kind of stress at some time.

Workers are affected by stress at work to different degrees. Most people will have had sleepless nights at some time, worrying about some aspect of their work; many people will have suffered from headaches or indigestion when they were feeling tense or anxious at work; or, again, who hasn't felt intensely angry and resentful with someone else at work? Or who hasn't come home from work at some time feeling tired, fed-up and irritable? All these complaints may seem fairly minor but they do demonstrate that stress is endemic in most people's working lives.

However it is also important to realise that a long period of exposure to stresses at work can have much more severe consequences for a worker's health and wellbeing. Some of these possible consequences are listed in the third column of Table 1. The stresses of work are thus in their own way dangerous like other hazards at work, including the biological, physical and chemical hazards that are dealt with in the other books in this series. Chapter 2 discusses some of the ways in which stresses at work can contribute to physical disease, to mental ill-health and to disruptions of social and family life.

The stresses of work can be counteracted. This book looks at some of the more important stresses and each one is briefly described. It explains the ways in which workers are affected, and finally, some ways of improving the situation are discussed.

The following common sources of stress are examined:

- **Low pay** Inadequate earnings mean that workers are unable to feed, clothe and house their families as they would wish. Their leisure, social life and family life can suffer as they become dependent on excessive overtime, or on shift bonuses to make ends meet.

- **Incentive payment systems** Incentive payment systems can enforce increasingly intense rates of work and an ever faster pace of production. They can sacrifice safety as workers are paid for speed and not for safe working, and they can produce anxiety, fatigue, friction and rivalry among those involved.

- **Shiftworking** Shiftworking involves the disruption of a worker's normal pattern of biological, psychological and social functioning. It conflicts with the normal rhythms of the body, can cause chronic fatigue, and play havoc with family and social life.

- **Job design** Modern production systems are organised to divide jobs into smaller and smaller elements, requiring less and less skill to perform, providing little or no job satisfaction but subjecting the worker to the rigid control of machinery. Such jobs have been effectively 'dehumanised'.

- **Work organisation** Modern work organisation is geared to a hierarchy of authority where the levels above direct and control the activities of the people below, often subjecting them to authoritarian supervision. Hierarchies often produce conflict and tension among those who work in the organisation.

It is important that shop stewards and safety representatives understand these stresses and how they can produce strain and ill health. They should be able to recognise the symptoms produced by stress, and they must be able to find ways of alleviating stress at work. This book provides some suggestions on how they should go about this.

2 Stress and health

This chapter looks at some of the ways in which stresses at work affect those who are exposed to them, and at how exposure to these stresses over a long period of time can have seriously harmful effects on the worker's physical health and psychological and social well-being. In this chapter we will focus on the general relationship between stress and health. Later chapters will look at the more specific ways in which particular types of working situations give rise to particular problems.

Psychological reactions to stress

Certain feelings and emotions are typically experienced by people under stress:

Fatigue

Perhaps the most straightforward experience of strain is tiredness. This may be due to overwork or lack of sleep or to the draining effect of emotional conflicts. When tiredness is pronounced and persistent and begins to interfere with work and other activities it is known as **fatigue. Exhaustion** is an extreme state of fatigue. Generally, fatigue is experienced as a feeling of dullness and drowsiness, as feeling clumsy and heavy and wanting to lie down. It becomes difficult to think clearly and to concentrate, and it becomes difficult to maintain attention on the task at hand. It is often accompanied by stiffness in the muscles and joints, aches and pains, and sometimes dizziness.

Anxiety

Anxiety is one of the most common reactions to stress. Part of the anxiety may be a fear that something unpleasant is likely to happen; for example that there will not be enough money to pay the rent, or fear of a conflict with a supervisor.

The anxiety may also reflect more general worry about work,

particularly when there are the pressures of too much work to do, when the pace of work is too great, or where there are a series of impossible deadlines which have to be fulfilled. Fatigue will often make the anxiety worse, making it more difficult to cope with the pressures. Very often the feeling of tension and unease that accompanies anxiety can begin to affect all areas of a worker's life. The anxiety can become more than just a worry or a fear that something is going to happen, and begins to become a permanent feeling of nervousness, unease and strain.

Anxiety tends to interfere with concentration and attention, and often prevents decisions from being made. An anxious person can be very sensitive and over-react very strongly to any slight threat or criticism, or be easily startled. Anxiety is also accompanied by muscular tension and sweating; and sleep is often disturbed – which in turn contributes to fatigue.

Depression

One of the results of **chronic** or permanent fatigue and anxiety can be increasing feelings of dejection, sadness and apathy. This is particularly true when it is not possible to see any way out of a stressful situation, and this gives rise to feelings of hopelessness, helplessness and personal inadequacy. This **syndrome**, or collection of feelings, is called **depression**. In some cases anxiety plays a large part in the depression and will show itself in feelings of agitation and in loss of sleep. In other cases anxiety is not an important factor and the depressed person may sleep an abnormally great amount and become generally rather listless and lethargic. A loss of appetite, and of sexual desire, and an increasing tendency to avoid other people and social situations are also common characteristics of depression.

Depression can be precipitated by a major failure, disappointment, or loss (like the death of someone close). In some cases the depression may persist for months after the episode which sparked it off.

Hostility and aggression

Feelings and attitudes towards others can also be affected by stress. Everyone will have had the experience of feeling irritable and losing one's temper when feeling tense, anxious, tired or under pressure. It is just a matter of degree before oversensitivity to others and irritability begins to make it difficult to relate to fellow workers, family and friends, without having constant rows and arguments. Particularly where a worker feels trapped in a situation that is increasingly difficult to cope with, it becomes more likely that feelings of resentment will build up and be directed at others who may not be to blame.

Such feelings of hostility and aggression are frequently not expressed to the person to whom they are directed. They thus become a permanent source of tension and resentment which is given no release. Occasionally there may be an outburst of very violent feelings during periods of particular tension. However such feelings are just as likely to be taken out on someone else who is quite innocent.

Psychosomatic complaints

Psychological stresses do not only affect moods and behaviour, they also affect the functioning of many parts of the body. These physical complaints which are due to emotional tensions are called **psychosomatic**. Amongst the most common psychosomatic complaints are headaches, backaches and muscle cramps, indigestion, and disturbances of sleep, or complete inability to sleep (**insomnia**). Tension and anxiety are particularly important factors in causing these complaints, though any strong emotion (such as frustration, resentment, or aggression) which has been prevented from being expressed may well show itself in psychosomatic disorders. The section on stress and health in this chapter discusses some of the more serious psychosomatic diseases.

Of course, not all headaches, aches and pains are caused by emotional factors. There are also many biological reasons for these complaints. This is also true of the stress-related diseases discussed in this chapter — hypertension, heart disease, ulcers, diabetes etc. It is certainly not true to say that all cases of these diseases are due to stress but stress may contribute to their development.

Neurosis

The changes in a person's mood, dispositions and behaviour discussed above can become sufficiently pronounced as to start disturbing relationships with others, and can begin to undermine confidence that one is leading a reasonably contented and trouble-free life. **Neurosis** is a general term for a range of mental or emotional disorders which, though serious, are not so severe as to involve a complete disorientation and loss of contact with reality.

Many neurotic states, like chronic anxiety, may appear entirely irrational and unjustified. However the neuroses discussed here are often a reaction to stress at work. Frequently such reactions will be made more extreme by factors outside of work like domestic problems or bereavement. Very often these neurotic states will affect other areas of life as well as what happens at work.

Control over the situation

Many of these neuroses develop precisely because the individual worker concerned has very little control over the situation he or she is in, and can see no possibility of doing anything to change it. The very fact of being able to take some positive action to counteract the stress will make for a more positive and 'healthy' mental state. However feelings of powerlessness and helplessness will only add to a developing anxiety and depression. A worker may find it impossible to cope with the stress either because there is no time or opportunity for rest or recuperation, or because it is impossible to escape from the contradictory demands of the situation.

For example, the pressures of excessive work loads often lead to working very long hours. Long hours restrict social contacts and leisure interests and leave no time for rest and recuperation. The heavy domestic responsibilities of many working women cause a similar problem – no opportunity to recover from work. Such people may have the constant feeling that there is always more work than is possible to finish – producing chronic fatigue and anxiety, and perhaps, insomnia (which will make the fatigue and anxiety worse). This in turn may lead to more pronounced character changes like depression or aggression.

Having a job which is disliked, but which demands constant high levels of attention and effort is one example where contradictory demands of the job cannot be resolved. In many other ways jobs can make demands which are impossible to fulfill, or which are quite incompatible with other demands which are equally strong. Pressures like this can lead to chronic anxiety, severe emotional tension and feelings of inadequacy, which may in turn lead to insomnia or depression or to psychosomatic disorders.

Overload and underload

The symptoms we have just described are probably most apparent in situations where some aspect of work is placing excessive demands upon the worker, whether it be the pressure of an excessive workload, a row with a supervisor, or whatever. But quite the contrary situation can also be highly stressful – work which is monotonous, routine and repetitive, which does not use any of the worker's skill, interest or initiative, and which prevents meaningful social contact with fellow workers. Such situations lead to boredom, frustration and isolation. Very often the stress of both overload and underload are present in the same job, as when work which is inherently unstimulating is done under great pressure of time and demands considerable attention. Chapter 6 will explore some of the consequences of this type of situation. One of the major effects of work which is unstimulating and unsatisfying is an impoverishment of mental health.

Mental health

Having good mental health is not just a question of not suffering from any particular neuroses or mental disorders – it is more a question of one's general attitude and feelings about one's self, the work that one does and about life in general. Thus, for example, someone with good mental health would not habitually tend to think that he or she was an inadequate or worthless person, or incompetent and lacking in ability. He or she would not always feel mistrustful of others and find it difficult to maintain friendly relationships, and would not tend to feel habitually dissatisfied, anxious and insecure. A high level of mental health would be characterised by the absence of, or the opposite of, these feelings.

Work fulfills a number of important psychological needs, as well as being a source of money. If these needs are not satisfied then this will affect the general psychological wellbeing of the worker. In general the following characteristics of work have been thought to promote good mental health.

- Having some kind of personal say or control over the work. This is particularly important in relation to the work process itself, but having some influence over the terms and conditions of employment, or general management decisions can also be important.

- Having work which is meaningful and interesting. This essentially means that work should involve a certain amount of skill, and contain some possibility for learning and development, and that it should be possible for a worker in any particular job to see how it fits into the total production process creating something which is socially useful.

- Having some degree of social contact and fellowship with other workers. Many people find their friends through meeting them at work.

The importance of work to maintaining workers' psychological health is highlighted by the demoralisation which often accompanies long-term unemployment. This demoralisation is characterised by feelings of apathy, inferiority and submissiveness.

But many working environments, including those with relatively high wages and fringe benefits may still be psychologically and socially unrewarding. In fact such work may seem like a trap, stopping any possiblity of self-fulfillment or social relationship with others at work – leading to the same feelings of apathy, inferiority, anxiety and depression. Such negative attitudes about one's self and one's life and work are, essentially, what is meant by poor mental health.

Family and social life

The psychological reactions described in the previous section inevitably affect relationships with others. Conflicts between people are often the cause of stress at work (see Chapter 5) but the tension, irritability, and aggression that stress engenders will tend to promote further conflicts with other workers, or with family or friends outside of work. Chronic fatigue and depression are often associated with sexual disturbances (like a loss of desire, or impotence) which in turn are a powerful source of conflict.

Social isolation

Shiftwork or excessive overtime means that workers do not have their time off with the rest of society. This makes it difficult to maintain a regular social life or to take part in social activities (including trade unions, clubs, societies or political parties), and can curtail family life as well. Further, it takes many workers several hours to relax and recover from the stresses and pressures of their work. This is time when they cannot interact normally with their families – they are too tired, tense or irritable. The longer term effects of stress on mood and general disposition are often accompanied by a gradual withdrawal from social relationships resulting in increased social isolation. Those relationships which do remain become increasingly superficial.

Social roles

Many aspects of work prevent workers from fulfilling their family and social roles as they would like to. Working parents frequently feel that they are not spending enough time with their children, particularly if child care facilities are not very good. Similarly for workers on low incomes, their role as a breadwinner or general provider is frequently under threat. This is even more so for those who are unemployed. Men frequently feel that being the main provider is an essential part of being a father and a husband, and having no work is a huge blow to their self-respect, causing great strains within the family, as well as considerable withdrawal from social contacts outside the family.

Physiological response to stress

We have looked at the effects of stress on mental health and well-being. We have seen how it can contribute to, or bring about, mental ill-health. But stress also harmfully effects our physical health as well.

The emergency response

When faced with an acute stress, the body's energy resources are mobilised to provide an immediate and effective response to that threat. The body's emergency response is designed to provide the *maximum* amount of energy to the brain and muscles in the *minimum* of time to ensure that the body is prepared for intense activity carried out in the most intelligent manner. Some of the main bodily changes involved in the 'emergency response' are outlined in Figure 1. The main changes involve increasing the amount of energy-giving glucose and oxygen in the blood, increasing the flow of blood, directing this supply to the brain and muscles, and slowing down all non-essential processes like digestion.

The release of glucose and free fatty acids (both of which, when combined with oxygen, produce energy for the heart and muscles) is under the control of various hormones which are secreted by the pituitary and adrenal glands. Figure 2 illustrates this process. It is possible to measure these hormones in the blood stream or when they are excreted in the urine. This has come to be one of the most reliable methods of measuring the body's response to stress.

Work situations which consistently evoke this stress or emergency response will drain the body's energy reserves while keeping

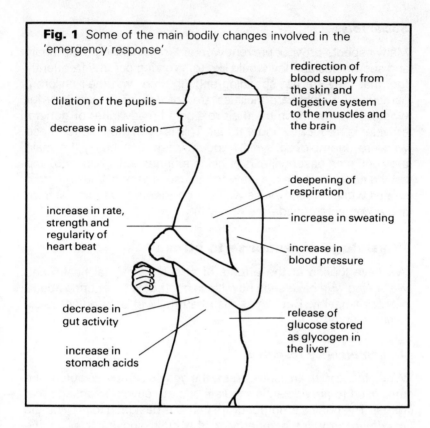

Fig. 1 Some of the main bodily changes involved in the 'emergency response'

dilation of the pupils

decrease in salivation

redirection of blood supply from the skin and digestive system to the muscles and the brain

deepening of respiration

increase in rate, strength and regularity of heart beat

increase in sweating

increase in blood pressure

decrease in gut activity

increase in stomach acids

release of glucose stored as glycogen in the liver

it in a state of excitation, which in turn prevents rest and the regeneration of these reserves.

Stress and disease

Although the emergency response is an adaptive response – the body is geared to cope with a severe threat – prolonged and repeated activation of the body in this way can lead to long-term degeneration of the body systems involved (particularly the blood circulation system) resulting in disease and ill-health. One of the main reasons why this degeneration occurs is because, although the 'emergency response' is geared to feeding the muscles with energy-giving substances, most stress situations don't demand a strong physical response which would use up this energy. Indeed many situations are experienced as particularly stressful precisely because there is no immediate way out, and the person involved is helpless and powerless to change the situation.

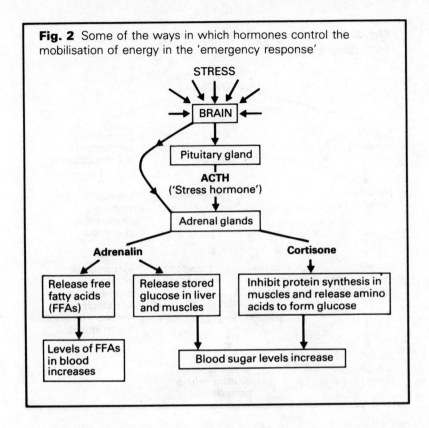

Fig. 2 Some of the ways in which hormones control the mobilisation of energy in the 'emergency response'

The blood circulation system

There are a number of different ways in which stress experienced over a long period of time can cause disorders and damage in the heart and blood circulation system, and which can lead to coronary heart disease. These are summarised in Figure 3 which is explained in more detail below.

Blood pressure

One of the main components of the 'emergency response' is an increase in blood pressure. When the body is prepared for intense muscular exertion this is due to the heart pushing a much larger volume of blood through the arteries to the muscles. However in stress situations which don't require this muscular activity, there is very often no great change in the volume of blood circulation, but there is an increased resistance to the blood flow caused by a

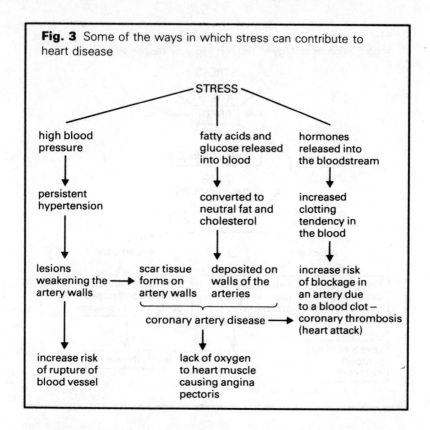

Fig. 3 Some of the ways in which stress can contribute to heart disease

STRESS

- high blood pressure
  - ↓
  - persistent hypertension
    - ↓
    - lesions weakening the artery walls →
      - ↓
      - increase risk of rupture of blood vessel

- fatty acids and glucose released into blood
  - ↓
  - converted to neutral fat and cholesterol
    - ↓
    - scar tissue forms on artery walls → deposited on walls of the arteries

- hormones released into the bloodstream
  - ↓
  - increased clotting tendency in the blood
    - ↓
    - increase risk of blockage in an artery due to a blood clot – coronary thrombosis (heart attack)

coronary artery disease →
  - ↓
  - lack of oxygen to heart muscle causing angina pectoris

narrowing of the blood vessels. However, once again this results in an increase in blood pressure.

In most circumstances, after the stress has passed the blood pressure will return to normal. However very often stress persists for a long time, as, for example, when the strain is experienced as chronic anxiety about work, or persistent feelings of hostility or aggression (which may never, or only rarely, be expressed directly). In these circumstances raised blood pressure levels (a condition known as **hypertension**) can last for years. In many cases, of course, when the stress is eventually removed blood pressure levels will return to normal, but it is also possible that the body will adapt to the prolonged high blood pressure levels and the hypertension will persist.

Over the short-term high blood pressure levels are nothing to worry about. However hypertension is a major factor leading to **coronary heart disease** or **strokes** (a rupture of a blood vessel in the brain), both of which can be fatal or severely disabling. This is because high blood pressure places a strain on the walls of the blood vessels. Tiny splits or lesions in the tissue appear and in the long-term they weaken the blood vessels and make them liable to burst under the strain. The healing of these tiny lesions can cause further problems – they create scar tissue and other deposits which then begin to constrict the flow of blood through the artery.

Coronary artery disease

The thickening and hardening of the coronary arteries, which is called **coronary artery disease**, is also caused by the deposits of fats and cholesterol forming on the walls of the arteries.

Psychological stress can contribute to this process in the following way. If the raised levels of fatty acids (released into the blood-stream as part of the 'emergency response') are not used up by muscular exertion they can be converted to neutral fat and cholesterol. This is laid down on the walls of the arteries making them narrower and restricting the flow of blood. Under these circumstances, when the heart is working particularly hard (as during physical exercise or periods of stress) the flow of blood can be insufficient to keep the heart muscle supplied with oxygen. When this happens a severe pain in the chest (often spreading to the shoulder and left arm) is experienced. This is known as **angina pectoris**. The pain will usually disappear after the exertion or stress passes.

Coronary thrombosis (heart attack)

When the arteries have been clogged and narrowed they are also more susceptible to a complete blockage from a blood clot. Hormones released into the bloodstream during the emergency response are known to increase the clotting tendency in the blood, and will therefore increase the likelihood of a blockage. A blockage in an artery supplying blood to the heart will cause painful damage to that part of the heart supplied by the artery and can often lead to complete heart failure.

A number of different factors can contribute to the risk of developing coronary heart disease. Heavy smoking is one long-term factor because it reduces the amount of oxygen the blood can carry. The fact that smoking is a common response to stress just serves to increase the strain on the heart. A diet rich in animal fats, and a lack of exercise also contribute because of their influence on the build-up of cholesterol in the bloodstream.

Coronary heart disease hardly ever occurs without some combination of the various processes we have been discussing – like hypertension, high levels of cholesterol, or oxygen starvation. However individual variation means that the heart and blood circulation systems of some people seem to be little affected by a lifetime in highly stressful situations.

However for those who are susceptible an acute coronary incident (heart attack) will tend to occur in circumstances like difficult interpersonal relationships, hard work and fatigue. It will often be precipitated by arguments or emotional upsets, unexpected exertion or sexual intercourse.

Other diseases

Hypertension and coronary heart disease are not the only serious diseases which are related to emotional strain and pressure. There is good evidence that diabetes may be precipitated in certain individuals by stressful situations. Diabetes is a disease in which lack of the hormone insulin prevents the body cells taking up glucose. Glucose is essential as an energy source for the body, and tissues cannot function without glucose entering the cells.

The incidence of **peptic ulcers** is also strongly related to emotionally conflicting situations. Feelings of anxiety, frustration, inadequacy and resentment increase the rate of gastric secretions (or at least upset the balance of different secretions in the digestive system) which in turn may lead to **ulceration**.

There is also evidence that various other diseases, including skin diseases and bronchial asthma, can be brought on by emotional conflicts, though the mechanisms through which this occurs as yet are not well understood.

Stress and drugs

Many workers turn to drugs to help them cope with the stresses of their work although this is not to say that all people who smoke and drink are using these substances as 'props'.

Such drugs include those like alcohol, tobacco and caffeine, which are generally socially approved for everyday use; those which are available through medical prescription (like certain tranquillisers and antidepressants); and those whose use is legally prohibited but are frequently available (like cannabis, LSD, and heroin). Any of these drugs can relieve some of the symptoms of strain; but, of course, none of them can remove the stress that is causing that strain. Thus alcohol or any of the tranquillising drugs can be very effective in inhibiting or counteracting anxiety and tension; antidepressants can give an emotional boost; heroin or LSD or cannabis can provide a temporary escape from the distressing reality into a state of euphoria, or of 'expanded consciousness'. However the need to keep taking these drugs will continue for as long as the person remains in the situation that is causing the strain. It is thus very easy to become psychologically dependent on such drugs and to come to rely on a regular dosage of a particular drug to get through a normal day's activity.

However, there are three main dangers in taking drugs as a way of dealing with stress. First, they can reduce the ability to function effectively at work or in domestic life. Alcohol can affect judgement and concentration and send you to sleep; tranquillisers cause doziness and lethargy. In fact any drug which affects mental processes can interfere with the ability to do one's job effectively, and this directly causes a build up of more and more pressure at work. It is easy to slip into a vicious circle with pressures at work leading to recourse to drugs, which increase the pressures at work because they make it more difficult to work effectively, which in turn leads to a higher or more frequent dosage of the drug and so on. You might find yourself drinking at lunchtime in order to be able to face the afternoon; but because you aren't able to do very much work in the afternoon you have so much more to do the next day; in the face of this pressure you may be even more likely to have a drink the next day.

Second, drugs affect safety at work. The connection between alcohol and road accidents is very well established, but the same principle applies with any drug which affects one's mental state and any work where the worker's (or any other person's) safety is affected by his or her judgement or decisions.

The third main danger of drugs is in physical dependence or addiction. The body will adapt to repeated dosage of many drugs. Very often it will become more tolerant. This means that the drug becomes less effective with repeated use, and larger and larger dosages are required to maintain the same effect. The body then often becomes physically dependent on the drug in the sense that it cannot function normally without it. When deprived of the drug the withdrawal symptoms can be extremely severe and occasionally fatal. Both alcohol and heroin are very addictive.

Individual susceptibility

- If shiftworking can damage the health of some workers why do other workers say they prefer shifts?
- When some people say they find working on an assembly line monotonous and soul-destroying, how can others in the same situation say they find their jobs interesting and challenging?
- Why do the pressures and conflicts of work contribute to chronic hypertension and heart disease in some workers, whereas others are not affected at all?

Workers differ greatly in their susceptibility to stress and in their ability to cope with the pressures and frustrations of their work. These differences are due to a whole range of factors – biological make-up, personal skills and abilities, interests and aspirations, social and domestic circumstances, and relationships at work. For example, just as some people are more resistant to colds than others, so people also differ in the likelihood of their developing coronary heart disease, or in being able to tolerate disturbances in their sleep–waking cycle caused by working shifts. Or, how well a job matches a worker's abilities and interests will of course determine whether work is stimulating and satisfying, or whether it demands either too much or too little in the way of skill or responsibility or judgement. Workers also differ in their personal and social circumstances. For many the satisfaction they can get outside work (in their hobbies or family life) compensates for the pressure and frustration of work and enables them to cope with these problems more adequately, whereas for others, stress and conflict in the domestic situation compound the problems they have at work. Similarly, mistrust and personal antagonism with colleagues at work can only increase the stresses and pressures of work, and undermine the worker's capacity to cope.

Is it possible then, simply to explain the effects of stress in terms of *individual susceptibility* and particular combinations of circumstances that make an individual vulnerable?

Frequently this means trying to select for particular jobs only those workers who can cope with the stresses involved in those jobs, and eliminating those workers who are likely to suffer some ill effects. There are several reasons why such an approach cannot be effective in eliminating the stresses at work.

First, it is impossible to select in advance only those workers who are not going to be adversely affected by stress — there is no way of telling until you put them into that situation. Frequently the effects of stress are very gradual and take a long time to develop. Thus people who initially seemed to be coping very well can, over a long period of time, suffer a gradual deterioration in health and well-being which may be difficult to reverse and which could not have been predicted earlier. It is of course possible to move workers from work which is causing them undue strain. This, however, leaves two problems. First, if those workers are not to suffer because they are susceptible, it is necessary to ensure their right of transfer to work of an equivalent nature, but which does not involve the same stresses. Second, other workers in the same situation, although they may not be affected to the same extent, are likely to suffer at least some of the effects of stress. If it is only possible to be transferred out of the situation if one is severely affected, then this guarantees that many workers will suffer.

For these reasons it is clear that a policy based on selection is one which tries to shift the responsibility for what are occupational illnesses on to the workers, and away from the organisational and environmental factors which are causing the problem. The only real solution is to work to remove the stresses which are causing the strain.

3 Pay, productivity and stress

Bargaining over how much workers produce and how much they are paid for their work is the central function of trade union organisation. For this reason our discussion of stress begins here.

In return for wages workers accept a whole range of working conditions and practices which affect the quality of their lives, their health and their general well-being. They do this within the context of employers attempting to maximise profitability and minimise labour costs. This quest for maximum profit for minimum outlay is the crucial factor determining the way work is organised, the technology and the social relations at work. It is thus the basis of many of the stresses discussed in this book.

Poverty and insecurity

Many factors help determine the market price of labour; but where bargaining power is limited workers will suffer from multiple stresses: low pay, job insecurity, a disproportionate dependence on overtime and shift premiums to maintain a living wage. Those at the bottom of the wage ladder also tend to suffer more than others from sickness and occupational accidents – and from what sociologists call 'social deprivation', affecting housing, education, family and social relationships. There are few aspects of the 'good life' for those who are poor. In fact, low pay threatens workers' ability to obtain even the necessities of life such as adequate food, clothing and shelter – and therefore continuously puts at risk the health and wellbeing of their families.

Not having any luxuries, having no savings for emergencies, 'rainy days' or holidays, never escaping from debts – all these can have effects beyond their immediate impact. Often they place a heavy burden on the very fabric of family life. Indeed poverty can be both cause and effect of family breakdown. Studies in America[1] have shown that low income families are twice as likely to break up as families on average incomes. The figures are probably very similar in Britain. Families which have broken up – single parents – are frequently poor.

Who are the low paid?

'Low pay' is obviously a relative term, and like all such terms it depends where comparisons are made. However there are at least four sections of the workforce which tend to be paid lower than the average. Despite the Equal Pay Act the average earnings of *women* remain far below those of men. *Immigrant* workers tend to be concentrated in the least attractive and lowest paid jobs. *Young* workers under the age of 21 – men, women, manual and white collar – all tend to be badly paid, and *older* workers, especially over the age of 50 in manual jobs begin to be less productive and become less able to meet the demands of shiftwork, bonus systems and overtime. As they become more dependent on basic rates their earning power falls.

However it is also necessary to look at people's earnings in relation to their needs, which are usually greatest during the middle years of their life when they have children. Although the earning power of workers may be greatest during these years, their earnings have to stretch much further. The earning power of families is drastically cut during this period if mothers leave work to look after their children. Thus the problem of low pay and poverty affect people at all stages of their lives.

Many of the low paid are concentrated in a number of low paying industries. Prominent amongst these are agriculture, clothing and footwear, distribution, food and drink, hotels and catering, and textiles.

The problems of the low paid

Besides the immediate impact of not having enough money to lead a healthy and fulfilling life, the low paid tend to suffer more from other problems relating to their jobs.

Job insecurity

Low paid jobs tend to have the least security of employment. Unemployment rates amongst the unskilled are $2\frac{1}{2}$ times the average. The unskilled and low paid tend to be the first hit in a recession. The anxiety caused by the constant threat of unemployment is very real – and the actual effect of being made redundant is often traumatic.

How severe the effects of unemployment are depends on a number of things, like how unexpected the job loss was and how long the person is without a job. Often the initial reaction to job loss is optimistic – about getting another job, and treating the time off as a holiday. However as the money runs short and no job is forthcoming this soon gives rise to anxiety and depression. Once in a state of depression a person feels lacking in energy, will spend a good deal of time lying in bed, which in turn leads to an acceptance of being unemployed; accompanied with feelings of apathy, inferiority and submissiveness.

Long periods of unemployment often cause particular problems for men because their inability to provide for themselves and their family threatens their self-respect and can lead to tremendous strains and tensions in the family, between man and wife and between parents and children.

Sickness

Those in low paid jobs tend to have higher than average rates of sickness absence from work. Unskilled workers have two or three times the amount of time off for sickness as professional or intermediate workers. Yet, despite this, fewer unskilled manual workers are covered by sick pay schemes than white collar workers, and the level of sick pay tends to be lower than that of white collar workers.

There are two main reasons for the higher level of sickness absence amongst low paid workers. On the one hand the jobs done by unskilled, low paid workers tend to be more dangerous and unhealthy – there is a greater chance of accident and occupationally related disease. On the other hand the low living standards of the low paid could make them less resistant to sickness and disease.

Overtime

The amount of overtime worked is highest among the low paid, and the majority of this overtime is regular. Regular and excessive levels of overtime can affect health, well-being and family life in the following ways:

- cutting down the time workers can spend with their families, for social life, hobbies or recreation.
- causing chronic fatigue. This means more than just feeling tired at the end of the day, but waking feeling tired, feeling tired throughout the day and becoming increasingly depressed and irritable.
- increasing the risk of having an accident. The rate of industrial accidents has been found to increase with long hours of work.

In snort, the more time spent at work the less time there is to recover from any stressful or toxic factors at work.

Incentive payment systems

Incentives have been traditionally regarded by management as one of the chief means of increasing productivity. For workers used to low pay it is often seen as a means of increasing earnings. In Britain 40% of male industrial workers receive some form of PBR (Payment By Results).

Table 2 illustrates the extent of the dependence on PBR and other 'additional' pay items in making up the weekly pay packet. For the average wage earner in British industry 25% of the pay packet comes from additional payments.

Table 2 Make-up of pay of male manual workers in selected industries

	Average gross weekly earnings			
	Total	of which		
		Overtime pay	PBR pay	Shift, premium pay
All industries and services	£80.7	£11.6	£7.2	£2.4
Mining and quarrying	£101.8	£15.7	£11.8	£2.6
Paper, printing and publishing	£88.4	£13.5	£5.0	£2.9
Transport and communications	£83.7	£16.2	£3.6	£3.5
Textiles	£73.7	£9.5	£7.2	£3.5
Public administration	£68.7	£7.9	£7.4	£1.0
Clothing and footwear	£67.3	£4.4	£14.6	£0.4

Source: *New Earnings Survey*, Department of Employment, 1978

Piecework establishes a direct relationship between the amount you get paid, the amount you produce and the speed at which you work. In practice how this operates depends very much on the balance of power on the shop floor. Everything will hinge on the level at which the rates for the piece are fixed.

Piecework is one of the most common factors causing stress at work. This is because piecework:

- forces an ever faster rate of work;
- reduces the quality of work produced;
- increases the risk of accidents;
- affects relationships with workmates.

We shall look at each of these questions in turn.

Speed of work

Because earnings are related directly to how much each worker produces, piecework provides a natural incentive to work fast in order to maximise earnings. All piecework systems are based on a standard time for each piece, or a standard number of pieces to be produced per hour. In setting the rate for each piece there is the assumption that one should be able to earn an approximate sum each week. If workers start earning 'too much' there will be the inevitable pressures to cut the piece rate.

Major problems arise for workers where the time allocation per piece has to be exceeded in order to earn an adequate wage and where bargaining power is limited. There is the danger of getting trapped in a vicious circle where they are continually working faster to maintain their weekly wage, but the faster they work the more the rate per piece gets trimmed.

Some workers may be able to take continuous speed-up, but for others it can cause chronic fatigue. Some of the common symptoms of chronic fatigue are feeling constantly tired, insomnia and loss of appetite – symptoms known to us all (see Chapter 2). These symptoms tend to disappear after a period of rest away from work, but will reappear when the pressures of piecework are again encountered.

Pieceworkers tend to complain that piece work causes them distress, discomfort and feelings of strain. They feel rushed, fatigued and physically uncomfortable. Pieceworkers in low paid unskilled work have been found to be more anxious, to suffer more psychosomatic complaints, and to feel less satisfied with their lives because of the pressures of their work.[2] Controlled experiments have also found higher levels of hormones associated with the body's stress reaction when piecework is introduced as in the example below.

Figure 4 shows what happened when 12 women office clerks were paid by piece wages or by salary on alternate days. Piece wages were always accompanied by a significantly higher rate of excretion of adrenaline (one of the main stress hormones). Piece wages were also accompanied by more complaints of feeling hurried, and of fatigue, backache and other pains.

Quality of work

The introduction of piecework tends to result in a decline in the quality of work because piecework emphasises quantity and not quality. For many workers the continual pressure to produce faster

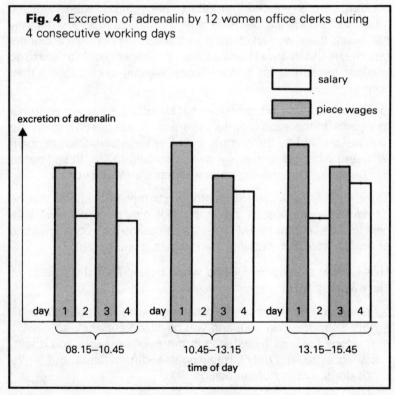

Fig. 4 Excretion of adrenalin by 12 women office clerks during 4 consecutive working days

Source: J. Fröberg et al, in Society, Stress and Disease, ed. L. Levi, Oxford, 1971

and faster with less and less attention paid to the quality of what they produce continually erodes pride in their work and diminishes their self-respect as workers.

Accidents

There is a clear relationship between the speed of production and the number of accidents – the faster the work is done and the more produced the more accidents occur. In one investigation of accidents in a goods despatch department, for example, there were 30 or more accidents a month in those months where over 2,500 vans were despatched, but only half of the number of accidents occurred when below 2,050 vans were despatched.[3]

A major strike by Swedish miners in the winter of 1969–70 demanded the end to piecework and its replacement by a monthly wage based on timed work only. The strike was successful and the change in the work system had a dramatic effect on safety. Severe accidents were reduced from 88 to 4 per year between 1969 and 1972; less severe accidents were also cut to a quarter of what they had been; there was an increase in the number of minor accidents reported – and this was because now the miners could afford to go and get treatment for minor injuries without risking losing their bonus.

In the construction industry payment by results is a major contributory factor to the accident rate. Where scaffolding is paid for by the 'square' and not by the number of safety ties, toe-boards or guard rails, and where trenches are paid according to length and not to the quality of the shoring, then accidents inevitably occur.

The British Safety Council recommends that PBR should not be introduced in hazardous industries. Not only does piecework increase the accident rate at work, it also makes for a constant state of anxiety through working in an unsafe environment.

This is how a London building worker described the effects of piecework in 1972:

> 'When you work, you have a pacemaker in front of you who gets £4 more than you, and you have to keep up with him. You look for bricklayers' jobs in the *Evening News* and it will say "greyhounds only", meaning speed merchants. But we're not dogs, we're human beings.'

Working relationships

It might seem that being paid in proportion to the amount you produce is about the fairest wage system you can devise, so why should it cause frictions, jealousies, anger and bitterness between workmates? The simple answer is that jobs differ and people differ. Because there is no accurate and exact way of fixing the rates for each piece there will always be 'good' jobs and 'bad' jobs, and who gets these and how they are shared out can be a source of rivalry and jealousy. Even where the payment system is based on the performance of the group as a whole there will be resentment at those who cannot keep up because of their effect on the group earnings level.

When the supply or flow of materials is held up, workers are dependent on whatever fall-back rates or waiting-time money has been negotiated. This will never be as much as the piece rate and leads to devisive friction between groups of workers.

Way back in the 1930s this is how the introduction of piecework at Morris Motors was described:

> 'Piecework did a lot to keep the men apart. Greed, how to get a bit more. And every department had one or two men who could work faster than the others. And you always had the cunning man who knew how to fiddle or get away with a job whereas another man couldn't, and he could soft soap the inspector, and he'd let his go and he wouldn't let mine go. Things like that. There was bitterness the whole time. You were keyed up all day. Tempers would get short, and sometimes a fight would break out. It was usually over work. Certain jobs were better paid than others, and men used to fight trying to get them.'[4]

Some forty years later the same problems exist.

Measured day work, productivity deals and stress

Despite all that has been said about piecework it is a system that can have considerable advantages for workers. The introduction of piecework can sometimes (but not always) mean an opportunity to increase earnings compared to what an hourly rate might offer. Furthermore, piecework can lead to greater *control* over the pace of work and earnings, though this will depend on the balance of power on the shop floor. So long as workers can negotiate rates that allow flexibility in the pace of work, they will have some control over the effort put into the job.

Thus with piecework there is the possibility of some **autonomy** and control on the shop floor because piece rates are up for negotiation. Also piece rates have been held responsible for 'wage drift' as actual earnings (based on locally negotiated piece rates) increase faster than basic rates (often negotiated on an industry-wide basis).

For these reasons measured day work has been introduced into many industries. **Measured day work** (MDW) takes away from the negotiating table the setting of time standards and puts them into the hands of management's work study engineers.

What is measured day work?

In MDW pay is fixed against a specified level of performance; this means that there has to be some form of work measurement and some way of monitoring the level of work performance achieved. Managements often argue that work measurement or work study is a science; being scientific involves being precise, accurate and impartial. Unfortunately work study does not meet this definition. The aim of work study is to set a performance standard that can be attained by 'someone who is qualified to follow a prescribed method by working at a normal working pace which can be sustained throughout a normal working day without undue fatigue and complying with prescribed quality standards'.

The measurement of a worker's performance times by the work study engineer is probably the simplest and least controversial part of the whole process. But arriving at the final standard time for the job involves a wide range of problems including:

- The choice has to be made of the 'average' worker whose performance is to be measured.
  Problem: Normal sustained working rates vary enormously from worker to worker.
- Measured time has to be converted into basic time by estimating the amount of effort produced by the worker in completing the job measured.
  Problem: Controlled studies have shown that effort rating is an unreliable process with variations of 20%–80% between raters.
- Basic time is converted to standard time by building in allowances for personal needs, fatigue, delays etc.

Problem: Again there are wide variations in assessing allowances.

- More and more firms are using 'synthetic' times taken from other work studies, rather than their own work measurement. *Problem:* Conditions in your workplace may not be the same as those from where the synthetic times are taken.

Measured day work means continuous pressure to keep up with a rate of production over which *workers have no control.*

What this amounts to is that under the guise of 'science' and 'work study engineering', MDW is a method of increasing production without increasing labour costs. The limits of the scheme are not scientific judgements, but shop floor revolt — spontaneous or organised. In order to control the pace of work it is therefore vital to see all the aspects of work as coming under joint union-management regulation, in other words as a matter of negotiation or of 'mutuality'. An essential aim therefore, is to ensure the membership can vary the pace of work and secure any free time created — not to allow management to take it away as 'wasted time'.

Productivity deals

Work measurement exercises and MDW are often introduced as part of an all round productivity deal, but such a deal often involves far more than the setting of standard work times. There is always the danger in productivity bargaining of 'selling off' various features of working arrangements which guarantee a certain amount of control, autonomy or flexibility. The proposed 'more efficient' arrangements may look fine on paper, but in practice they may mean that more time is spent working under pressure. Thus it is important to assess the quality of the job as a whole before consenting to the elimination of rest breaks, or the restriction of manning levels, or other changes.

The introduction of shiftwork and/or new technology and machinery are often components of a productivity deal and these form the subject of the next two chapters.

References
1 *Work in America*, MIT, 1973.
2 Gardell, B. in *Society, Stress and Disease*, Vol. 1, L. Levi ed. Oxford University Press, 1971.
3 P. Powell et al., *Two Thousand Accidents*, National Institute of Industrial Psychology, 1971.
4 A. Excell in *History Workshop* 6 p. 56, 1978.

4 Shiftwork and stress

Shiftworkers have to work at some time other than the normal working day – either at night, in the evenings or in the early mornings. This means that their daily work and rest pattern is always in conflict with the normal daily activity cycle of their body and the pattern of work, rest and leisure of their family, friends and the rest of the community. This conflict can have serious consequences for their health and well-being.

Types of shiftwork

According to an estimate by the General and Municipal Workers Union (GMWU) there were in 1979 at least 3 million full-time workers in the UK employed as shiftworkers. But the true extent of shift and unsocial hours working remains unknown. Some estimates place the figure for all workers, including part-timers, as high as 6 million.

The most intensive shift working sectors include transport, post and telecommunications, the Health Service, electricity supply, coal mining, metal manufacture, chemicals, glass, rubber, textiles, food and drink, and vehicles.

There are many different shiftworking systems operating in British industry, but the majority fall within the following categories:

- *Systems without night work*
  Two-team ('double days')
  (a) Nonoverlapping (e.g. 06.00–14.00, 14.00–22.00 hrs)
  (b) Overlapping (e.g. 06.00–14.00, 13.30–21.30 hrs)
- *Systems with night work*
  Two-team (up to 12 hour shifts) ('days and nights')
  Three-team (8 hour shifts)
  One-team (night work only) ('permanent night shift'): this is often combined with 'double days' to provide complete coverage of the 24 hour period.

- *Systems with night work and including weekend work* ('continuous shift work')
  (a) Three-team (12 hour shifts)
  (b) Four-team (8 hour shifts)
  (c) Irregular (varying number of teams and cycle lengths)[1]

Shifts also vary according to their **rotation period** and **rotation direction**. The rotation period is the number of consecutive days on the same shift. Less than seven days on the same shift is counted as a short rotation period, more than seven days is a long period. A regular rotation direction has the following sequence of shifts: morning, afternoon, night; while an inverse rotation gives a sequence of morning, night, afternoon. Inverse rotations do not allow enough rest when changing between certain shifts. Regular rotations of three shifts do allow a 24 hour gap between shift changes

Table 3 shows the burden of unsocial hours worked in various patterns of shiftworking.

Table 3 Unsocial hours associated with patterns of work, 1979

	Type of work pattern				
	Day work	Double days	3-shift non-cont.	3-shift cont.	Permanent nights
No. of days worked in 1979	233	233	233	247	233
Total unsocial hours in shift	Nil	504	1087	1351	1864
As a % of total hours worked	—	36.8	58.3	68.3	100
No. of public holidays worked	Nil	Nil	Nil	7	Nil
No. of Saturday/ Sundays worked	Nil	Nil	Nil	71	Nil
No. of morning shifts	Nil	121	77	91	Nil
No. of afternoon shifts	Nil	121	79	82	Nil
No. of night shifts	Nil	Nil	77	74	233

Source: GMWU Research Department, 1979

The effects of shiftwork

Shiftwork affects health and wellbeing in two main ways: it conflicts with the biological rhythms of the body (particularly those of sleeping and digestion), and it disrupts family and social life.

Biological Rhythms

Many bodily functions follow a marked daily pattern of activity. The sleep-waking cycle is one of the most obvious and important; but this daily cycle of quiesence and activity can be measured in many other ways, for example by measuring body temperature and the levels of various hormones which are important to the functioning of the body. The level of physiological activity increases during the waking hours and declines as the time for sleep approaches. Figure 5 shows the typical variations in adrenaline secretion and body temperature over a 48 hour period. The body temperature rhythm lags behind the adrenaline rhythm by about 2–3 hours. Adrenaline is one of the most important hormones which control the level of physiological activity. Body temperature reflects this activity.

The bodily process involved in digestion and excretion also has a strong daily rhythm, as do many other physiological functions which affect the way we feel and behave. These biological rhythms are mainly synchronised to our social environment (what everyone else in the community is doing) and to our awareness of

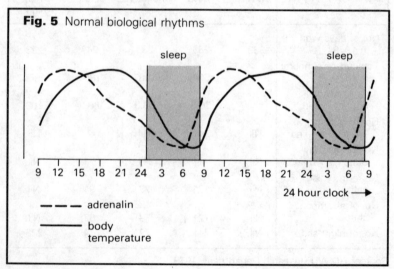

Fig. 5 Normal biological rhythms

sleep   sleep

9 12 15 18 21 24 3 6 9 12 15 18 21 24 3 6 9

24 hour clock →

– – – adrenalin

——— body
temperature

what time it is. They are resistant to change and only adapt slowly to changes in a worker's pattern of working, sleeping, and eating. During the working week biological rhythms might begin to adapt to the shift pattern, but during rest days they will very rapidly revert to the normal pattern of the worker's family and the community, so the process of adaptation has to begin again.

Sleep

Working at night inevitably means sleeping during part of the day, and this affects both the quantity and quality of sleep.

The quantity of sleep

For shiftworkers, sleep during the day is virtually always shorter than sleep during the night; typically day sleep is between one and two hours shorter. This difference between day and night sleep holds despite the fact that people's sleep requirements vary considerably. As you get older you tend to need less sleep – but even so the sleep of older workers is still shorter when taken during the day than it is during the night.

The quality of sleep

As well as the length of sleep the quality of sleep tends to be worse during the day than at night. As we sleep we go through a regular succession of sleep stages, alternating between lighter and deeper sleep and 'dreaming' sleep. While the sequence of sleep stages seems to remain the same in day sleep, the amount of 'dreaming' sleep is diminished. It is this 'dreaming' sleep which is thought to have particularly important recuperative effects.

The biological rhythms which gear the body towards activity and wakefulness during the day, ensure that day sleep tends to be lighter and more fitful than night sleep. In short, sleep during the day is shorter and less 'good' than night sleep.

Interruptions of sleep

Day sleep is more often interrupted than night sleep. Nightworkers still feel hungry during the day and often get up for a snack or for a regular mid-day meal. Day sleep is also more frequently interrupted by having to get up and go to the toilet. Then again, trying to sleep when the rest of the community is geared to being awake and active, results in sleep being disturbed by noise – from children, from traffic, from the telephone ringing, from regular callers, casual visitors, and so on. One of the most frequent complaints of shiftworkers is that noise disturbs their sleep during the day.

The sleep debt

What are the effects of the inadequate sleep pattern of the shiftworker? Trying to get sufficient good sleep tends to be a major preoccupation of shiftworkers. When the rotation period is fairly long and several consecutive nights are spent working, they tend to build up a 'sleep debt' – they suffer more and more from inadequate sleep with each successive day. They can only make up for this 'sleep debt' by sleeping for abnormally long periods during their days off. And as the working week progresses and the sleep debt accumulates, they feel increasingly tired, listless, nervous and irritable. On average approximately 20% of shiftworkers find it impossible to continue working shifts because they just cannot get enough sleep.[2]

However, many more than this have some problems with their sleep and in general as workers get older the problems become worse. One study has found that while 17% of workers under the age of 25 had sleep disorders, over 70% of workers over 40 did. In various studies between 50% and 62% of shiftworkers have been found to suffer from sleep disorders, compared to between 5% and 11% of day workers.[3]

Digestion and appetite

Getting adequate regular meals at times when they feel like eating is another major problem for shiftworkers. Working at night usually means eating at night, and this is a time when their body is not used to coping with food – the digestion processes are geared to a period of quiescence and sleep.

In addition to this canteen facilities and the quality of food on the night shift are often greatly inferior to those on the day shift, if they exist at all. Rotating shift schedules make it very difficult to plan and organise regular meals; this means that many shiftworkers end up by missing one or more meals a day, particularly breakfast but also lunch. Others find themselves eating an extra meal, and this overeating puts an additional strain on the digestive system and can lead to obesity.

The processes of digestion are also made more difficult by increased consumption of tobacco, caffeine and alcohol, all of which are known to have a harmful influence on digestion. On the night or early morning shift there is a greater tendency to smoke more tobacco and to drink more coffee in order to stay awake; and the disruption of social life tends to make shiftworkers drink more alcohol.

For all these reasons then it is not surprising that shiftworkers suffer from indigestion and general gastric disorders twice or three times more often than day workers. Bowel disorders – constipation, often in conjunction with haemorrhoids (piles), and colitis – are also associated with shiftwork and the difficulty of maintaining regular bowel functions. Some studies have also shown a much higher rate of ulcers among shiftworkers than day workers.

There are two ways of interpreting this association between shiftwork and digestive ulcers. On the one hand the ulcers might be due directly to the irregularity of eating and the disruption of digestive processes already discussed. On the other hand the ulcers might be 'psychosomatic' – that is, due to the excessive fatigue, stress, worry and anxiety caused by the general personal and social disruptions that are the inevitable result of shiftwork. Both these factors are probably important in causing the ulcers. It is interesting to note that the ex-shiftworkers in one Norwegian study also suffered from high rates of nervous disorders. We will return to this topic after discussing performance and accidents.

Fatigue, performance and accidents

It is not only sleeping and eating which follow a strong regular rhythm resistant to the demands of shiftwork. Most of our other important mental and physical processes fluctuate and vary throughout the 24 hour cycle in a way which is resistant to change and to which the body finds it difficult to adapt. Thus when we are awake at night we tend to feel drowsy and lethargic, our body temperature falls and other physiological processes slow down. Many shiftworkers suffer from chronic fatigue – they rarely feel alert, relaxed and attentive to what they are doing. Instead they feel tense, irritable, distractable, worn out and generally run down. Laboratory and industrial studies have shown that workers tend to make more errors and work at a slower rate on the night shift.

Surprisingly, not all studies show that the rate of industrial accidents is higher on the night shift. Studies which have looked at the severity of accidents have tended to show that whereas all accidents tend to be more frequent during the morning shift, there are more severe accidents on the night shift. In addition we know from experience that minor accidents on the night shift don't get reported as often as they do on the day shift.

For many shiftworkers working at night spells danger, and for most it means persistent fatigue, drowsiness and exhaustion. However, for many shiftworkers this is only the start of their problems as the disruption to the pattern and order of their lives can become a threat to their mental well-being.

Fatigue and mental health

The studies mentioned above found high rates of nervous disorders (which would include the symptoms described above) amongst ex-shiftworkers. Other studies have found that those actually working shifts have up to two and a half times more nervous disorders than day workers, and that both those on permanent nights and those working rotating shifts are affected.[4]

Unfortunately, not many of these studies have described in any detail what these 'nervous disorders' are actually like. However one pattern is fairly common, called **night worker's neurosis**. There are three main symptoms of this: feeling generally weak and listless, especially in the morning; insomnia (inability to sleep) combined with feeling tired and sleepy throughout the time one is awake; and disorders of mood and behaviour – particularly aggression, and depression (these are described in more detail in Chapter 2).

Fatigue and drugs

Having to work at a time when the body is geared towards sleeping, and having to sleep when the body is geared to activity tends to mean that work makes one overtired, and that one's sleep is not sufficiently good to provide rest and recovery to restore one's energies. In this situation it is very easy to slip into a vicious cycle of feeling tired yet unable to sleep; taking sleeping pills in order to get some sleep; feeling even less active and refreshed on waking; taking other, stimulant drugs before going to work, and more perhaps to keep going during the shift; then being unable to relax and sleep and taking larger doses of sleep-inducing drugs; and so on. It is not known how many shiftworkers take psychotropic drugs (drugs which affect mental activity), but the number is probably very large. Such drugs can be dangerous – particularly if taken when suffering from lack of sleep, or having drunk alcohol. They can affect performance and judgement and can lead to accidents.

Family life

Shiftwork is a frequent cause of disruption to family life. The shiftworker has a number of alternatives; to conform to the family's routine; to make the family conform to the shift routine, or to follow the shift routine more or less independently of the family. Either way it is difficult to avoid problems; three-quarters of one group of workers on a continuous three-shift system said that the disruption to family life was the worst and most inconvenient aspect of shiftwork. The problems are less severe on 'double-days' because the worker does not have to contend with the night shift. Rapidly rotating schedules make it more difficult to predict, plan and organise the preparation of meals, housework, shopping and the care of children. For many male shiftworkers it is their wives who make it possible for them to continue working shifts by organising their lives around the shift pattern. As with most workers home and family life is important as a stable base and source of support and relaxation.

> 'I don't get much family life – only at the weekend. I come home at about dinner time, the kids are at school; I have about half an hour with them when they come home, then I have my tea and go to bed. The wife goes to bed when I get up.'
> (permanent night worker)
>
> 'Working shifts has upset our relationship – you don't see each other, you don't have time to talk about things; it's one big rush – she's in – a quick meal and you're out – that's it. That's all you see of each other – an hour a day five days a week. It obviously affects your sex life – you can't wake your wife at five a.m.'
> (days and nights worker)

The problems of women shiftworkers are particularly difficult to resolve because the major burden of household work falls usually on them. They have to create the stable home as well as suffer the disruption of shiftworking. Office cleaners completing a seven hour shift at night might come home just in time to make breakfast for the family and get the kids off to school. After cleaning the house and shopping there might be time for only a couple of hours sleep in the afternoon before collecting the children and preparing the evening meal. Thus the dual exploitation of work and work at home is made that much more intolerable by shiftwork.

Just how shiftwork can affect family life will depend on individual circumstances. For example, if you have a small house and several children you are almost bound to have problems getting sleep during the day because of noise, and your need to sleep will interfere with your family's freedom to go about their normal activities. Thus you sleep badly and your family resents having to try to avoid disrupting you. It is situations like this which can lead to tension and conflict.

Marital relationships also suffer because of shiftwork. If both husband and wife work and one is on shifts (particularly when there is a long rotation period or permanent nights) there will be long periods when they will only be in the house at the same time for a couple of hours each day – it really becomes a weekend marriage. In this situation it is very difficult to find the time for relaxation together and companionship that can prevent a marriage becoming strained and difficult.

However it would be wrong to say that this is the whole story about shiftwork and family life, because many shiftworkers do find that it has some positive benefits. The main advantage is the possibility of having more free time to spend with families during the day, and this is particularly so if there are very young children at home.

Social life – 'social death'

Nearly every social and community activity is organised to fit in with normal working, leisure and sleeping patterns. Working shifts means not fitting into that pattern and it is for this reason that shiftworkers tend to feel isolated and cut off from their community; it's as if they are set apart in a separate social system. This has led to the use of the term **social death** to describe their situation.

Those who are young, single, and live alone are probably the most vulnerable to the social isolation caused by shiftwork. Indeed it has been recommended that such people should not take up shiftworking.

'You have no social life during the week; you accept that as part of the job.' (night worker)

'You can't get out at night; the wife has to stop in; you have to sleep on Saturday morning, so if you are starting days on Monday, Saturday afternoon and Sunday is your only break. It makes a short weekend.' (days and nights worker)

'It screws up your social life a bit, especially night work. It is difficult to go away at weekends because you need to get some sleep on Sunday afternoons.' (days and nights worker)

Individual susceptibility to ill health

Not all shiftworkers suffer ill-health due to working shifts; some are more susceptible than others. In one study of a Norwegian electro-chemical works there were 345 dayworkers, 380 shiftworkers and 128 former shiftworkers. The study showed that while both shiftworkers and dayworkers suffered from various disorders to the same extent, there were large numbers of ex-shiftworkers who suffered from much higher rates of digestive and nervous disorders (see table 4); it had been their inability to adapt to shiftwork that had caused them to give it up.

Table 4 Percentage of day workers, shiftworkers, and former shiftworkers who transferred to day work for medical reasons suffering from nervous and gastro intestinal complaints

Diagnostic class	Dayworker	Shiftworker	Former shiftworker
Nervous disorders	13.3	10.5	32.8
Verified peptic ulcers	7.1 ⎤	6.1 ⎤	18.0 ⎤
Peptic symptoms without demonstrable ulcer	6.7 ⎥ 25.2	10.0 ⎥ 26.3	11.7 ⎥ 50.0
Other gastro-intestinal conditions	11.3 ⎦	10.2 ⎦	20.3 ⎦

Source: Aanonsen A, *Shiftwork and Health*, Oslo 1964

There are two main implications of this study:
1 Shiftwork does contribute to digestive and nervous disorders in at least a proportion of shiftworkers. It is important that these workers are able to change their jobs to escape shiftwork. This

was obviously possible in this Norwegian works, but as other studies have shown, many workers remain in shiftwork despite ill-health.

2 Even if those who remain in shiftwork are reasonably healthy, many of those who give it up suffer and continue to suffer ill-health because of shiftwork.

Thus a process of self-selection for shiftwork does take place in that those who remain as shiftworkers can often tolerate it. However, very often people cannot afford to select themselves out of shiftwork. For many that do leave shiftwork it is only after their health has suffered.

Can one adapt completely to shiftwork?

In physiological terms the simple answer is no. As we have seen when we wake in the morning our physiological activity starts to increase, reaching a peak during the afternoon or early evening. It then slows down as the evening wears on and is at its lowest level during the night when we sleep. Adapting to night work would require this 'biological rhythm' to change so that the highest levels of activity are at night and lowest levels during daytime. But this adaptation rarely takes place, and there are two reasons for this. Firstly, even when working shifts, not all activity is geared to the artificial shift time; and we 'know' what the normal correct time is. So even when working shifts many of our activities are still tied to the normal community time, inevitably affecting our body's functioning.

Secondly, even if we were to alter all our activities to shift time during our working days, it would still take several days (and for some physiological responses, several weeks) for our body to adapt to the new time pattern. But every week during rest days the shiftworker's activity pattern changes back to the normal community time. The biological rhythms also rapidly revert to community time and the process starts again. Thus most of one's working time is spent in a state of no adaptation or semi-adaptation to shift time.

However, it must also be said that some people can cope better than others with the disturbances of their biological rhythms. Thus they find it relatively easy to sleep during the day and to arrange their meals at times which suit their shift. In general the younger you are the easier it is to cope. However, people usually don't 'get used' to shifts – the longer they work shifts, the more difficult it gets to cope. Older workers who have been working shifts longer are more likely to be affected by bad health, particularly due to problems of sleep and digestion. This explains why there is such a high turnover of labour on shifts.

Some people should not work shifts

Because older workers are so much more affected by working shifts many experts would recommend that workers should not start shiftworking if they are in their forties or fifties. And this is also why it is particularly important to prevent workers being 'trapped' in shiftwork as they get older and less able to cope. This means making it easy to transfer out of shiftwork to an equivalent job on permanent days.

Certain medical conditions are aggravated by the irregularities of the life of the shiftworker, and those who suffer from these conditions should avoid shiftwork. This would include those who have a history of digestive disorders, those who need to have regular food or regular medication (e.g. diabetics and those with thyroid trouble) and epileptics, because the sleep reduction tends to increase the incidence of fits.

> 'Night work, as at present practised, always causes fatigue and also, in many cases, a psychosomatic occupational disease (neuroses and digestive ulcers) to which the practice of rotation can add specific digestive disorders. Moreover, the mental load involved in a task and the ageing of the worker can constitute aggravating factors. Again, night work disturbs family and social life . . . Night work should be banned wherever its practice is motivated solely by the financial consideration of making costly equipment pay for itself more quickly.'[5]

Is there a 'good' shift system?

The short answer to this is no, and therefore it is better to avoid shift working if you have the choice. If you don't have the choice it may be possible to press for certain changes which may make shift working more tolerable. There is much discussion on whether short rotation periods of one or two days are better than longer periods of several weeks or even permanent nights. It is claimed that the longer the rotation period is, the more chance the body has to adapt itself to the shift routine. Other experts have claimed that because the body never really adapts no matter how long the rotation period, and because there will always be a conflict between shift time and normal time, it is better to have a fast rotation period so that the body stays locked into normal time. Then workers can try to recover from one or two night shifts during the following one or two days when they are working during the day. Long rotation periods also mean much longer periods of social isolation. On the other hand they make it easier to plan and organise a more regular social life for the times when they are free during the day or evening.

So however the shift systems are juggled it seems someone is going to lose out. But is there no way of making some of the harmful consequences of shiftwork less damaging? There are three things that might help. These are:

- a reduction in the amount of night work so that fewer workers are affected;
- a reduction in working hours for shiftworkers so that there is more time to recover from its effects;
- provision for early retirement for older shiftworkers, and for automatic right of transfer to permanent day work (without loss of earnings) for other shiftworkers.

The last point would ensure the right to transfer for those who have reached a certain age, or have been working shifts for a certain length of time, or have been certified as medically unfit for night work.

Because chronic fatigue and inadequate sleep are two of the main problems confronting shiftworkers, a drastic shortening of working hours is essential to allow adequate rest and recuperation after night work. This could take the form of fewer shifts per week, or shorter working shifts. Some experiments with shift systems in Sweden have been organised around a twenty-eight hour week (with either eight hour or six hour shifts). In France the trade unions are working for a progressive reduction of hours of work to 33 hours a week for night workers.

Organising the hours off should be guided by two principles. Firstly, sufficient time off should be guaranteed to ensure a good night's sleep between any two night shifts. This implies at least 24 hours' rest after each night shift. Secondly, a larger number of free weekends should be guaranteed than are currently allowed by most continuous shift systems. Preferably one weekend in two should be free. This would allow the worker to take part in a fairly regular family and social life and help alleviate the social isolation of working shifts.

If improvements meant higher manning levels on the night shift, thereby exposing more workers to the effects of night work, it would be essential to reduce the amount of work done at night by transferring to day time all preparatory work and any non-essential operations and processes.

Other arrangements which would ease the burden of working shifts include:

- Fast and efficient transport laid on at the beginning and end of each shift. For many shiftworkers travelling at unsocial hours increases the length of their shift because public transport is irregular or unavailable.

- Facilities on the night shift – including canteen, welfare, first aid, safety arrangements – should be at least as good as those on the day shift.

- Creche facilities should be provided for the young children of shiftworkers. The domestic responsibilities of women shift-workers are particularly difficult, and this would alleviate some of the hardship.

- There should be regular medical check-ups for shiftworkers. All workers starting shiftwork should have a full medical check; there should be another after the first six months working shifts, and annually after that.

- The work of shop stewards should be facilitated by ensuring that stewards from different shifts have the right to meet each other regularly in the firm's time. Night shift stewards should not have to come in during the day to meet management; they should be able to meet management during shift hours.

- Provision should be made for the retraining of shiftworkers to facilitate transfer to the day shift; a sufficient number of jobs on permanent days should be provided for those who wish or need to transfer to the day shift.

Legislation and shiftwork

In some countries, such as Belgium, Norway and Sweden, night work is banned, except where special exemptions have been made where both unions and employers agree that night work is essential. In Britain, women and younger persons (under 16) are protected from working between 8 p.m. and 7 a.m. by the Factories Act of 1961 (Part VI). Again exemptions can be made where both management and workers agree. Out of approximately two million women working in factories, nearly 200,000 are covered by exemptions allowing their hours to be extended, and over 30,000 are specifically exempted from protection against night work. Many women also work shifts in the service industries (life hospitals or cleaning) which are not covered by the protective legislation. There is pressure from bodies like the CBI to have this protective legislation repealed in the name of sexual equality. However it would be more sensible to extend the protection to men (Sweden did this in 1967). Women don't like doing night work any more than men do and its effects on their health and well-being are much the same. All the arguments point to equal protection for men and women from shiftwork.

The EEC Commission at one stage gave consideration to legislation controlling the amount of shiftwork, covering the right to return to day work, early retirement for shiftworkers, reduction in weekly hours of work or longer holidays, and the establishment of minimum rest periods between shifts. Sadly, employer resistance has led to the proposals being shelved.

References
1 Rutenfranz, J. et. al. *Scandinavian Journal of Work Environment and Health* 3 (1977) 165–182.
2 *ibid.*
3 *Night Work*, International Labour Office, 1978.
4 *ibid.*
5 *ibid.*

5 Social relations and psychological pressures at work

Hierarchies in organisations

Virtually every form of work organisation – in both private and public sectors – consists of a **bureaucratic hierarchy**. In such a hierarchy the work of each part of the organisation is divided into a set of rigidly defined jobs and individually specified by the particular work activities they involve, the power and responsibility that goes with them and the status they carry in the organisation. Each job fits into a finely graded pyramidal structure and workers at each level in the hierarchy are responsible to, and controlled by, those in the level above. Power and authority in the organisation is exercised on the basis of rigid rules which reflect the superior/subordinate system of the hierarchy.

In this chapter we explain in a little more detail some of the characteristics of hierarchies; we then examine some of the ways in which hierarchies create conflicts, tensions, and pressures at work and finally we look at how these conflicts and pressures can lead to disease and ill health.

Characteristics of hierarchies

The nature of the bureaucratic hierarchy determines the relationship of workers to their work. It sets limits to the worker's freedom to organise his or her work; it specifies certain endemic sources of conflict, and produces certain areas of frustration, anxiety and uncertainty.

Pyramidal structure

In a manufacturing enterprise, for example, the bottom level comprises production line workers, skilled craftsmen, and all those who carry out the tasks of constructing, creating, and assembling; in short, all those who either directly or through tools and machinery, work the raw materials into the finished product. Directly

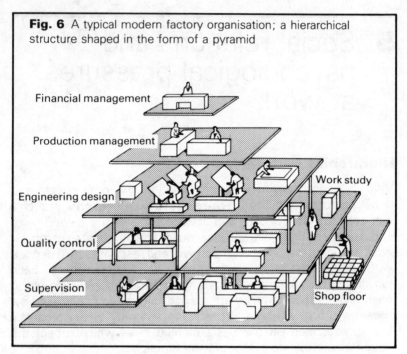

Fig. 6 A typical modern factory organisation; a hierarchical structure shaped in the form of a pyramid

Financial management

Production management

Engineering design

Work study

Quality control

Supervision

Shop floor

Source: *Industrial Democracy*, BBC Publications, 1976

supervising and controlling their work are foremen and first line supervisors. These in turn are controlled by the lower levels of production management, who in turn are directed and controlled by succeeding higher levels of management. At the top all are subject to the authority of the managing director or whoever exercises executive power at the apex of the hierarchy. He or she will, of course, be responsible to the owner(s) of the enterprise, in the furtherance of whose interests the whole structure is created and continues to function.

Division of work

The work of the organisation is usually divided into smaller and smaller independent units or tasks, each of which is allocated to one person, or one organisational unit, in such a way that the functions of each unit or person have clearly demarcated boundaries. There are also rules and programmes which relate and control the performance of each unit without the need for constant personal and direct supervision. Essentially it is a system where, as one Ford shop steward put it, 'their view was that we were paid to go there and wield a hammer, and they were paid to sit up in an office somewhere and do the thinking'.

Superiors and subordinates

There is one primary relationship between workers in the hierarchy – that is the **superior/subordinate** relationship. Basic to this relationship is the separation of those who make the decisions from those who carry them out. This is true at all levels of the hierarchy – the superior makes decisions and the subordinate must carry them out, and, except at the top and bottom of the hierarchy, each person is at the same time both a superior and a subordinate. It is also true that, because each superior is held responsible for the performance of his or her subordinates, the superior will tend to invade every possible area of discretion and autonomy of the subordinate.

In such situations superiors almost inevitably try and put pressure on their subordinates. 'I think there is a need for more pressure. People need to be needled a bit. I think man is inherently lazy and if we could only increase the pressure . . . budgets would be more effective.' This manager, quoted in a study of people at work,[1] sums up in clear terms a typical approach in modern bureaucratic hierarchies.

The bureaucratic hierarchy is a system where tight control over all areas of work is built into the structure of the organisation. It is a system where the greatest amount of discretion and control over work is removed from the worker and invested in the hierarchy. It is a system where loyalty to the company is enforced by an extended promotion system, in which the best way to improve your position is to adopt the ideals and values of the organisation as your own.

What are the consequences for those who work within this system?

Conflict between controllers and controlled

Production workers

There is the endemic conflict between the supervisors and controllers and those they supervise and control. At the most basic level there is the wearing effect of being continually subject to what is often petty and arbitrary discipline at work. One of the most frequent complaints is not being treated with dignity or 'like human beings'. Women workers find themselves particularly victimised by the power and authority of male supervisors because their subordinate role at work is compounded by the social inequalities that women suffer.

Foremen

The fundamental conflict between management and labour bears particularly heavily on foremen – the so-called 'men in the middle'. The foreman is at the front line of production supervision and as such is under constant pressure from higher management to maintain high production levels. In transmitting these pressures to the shop floor the foreman is the first to encounter any resistance from workers individually or collectively. However, the frustrations of the foreman's job arise because the very broad responsibilities of the job are not matched by an equivalent degree of decision-making power or control over the many factors that affect production. The foreman does not exercise final responsibility for deciding when a job is to be done, how it is to be done or to what standards, nor does he or she usually directly monitor quality. Yet the foreman is responsible for ensuring that production levels are maintained according to these decisions.

Many foremen manage the difficult and delicate job of satisfying production demands, while remaining sensitive and responsive to the pressures on workers and their individual problems. More often than not the foreman and supervisor are criticised by both management and workers, but get pushed aside when key decisions are to be made. Foremen are often made scapegoats for bad management decisions, and are open to public humiliation when their own decisions are reversed by higher management. As one shop steward put it: 'the supervisor gets kicked about from pillar to post. You know they're just used by management. They're told what to do . . . management put them up as a front and then when we push a bit management won't support them.'

Shop stewards

Managerial pressure to maintain or increase levels of production will produce pressures on workers, their shop stewards and union officials.

Shop stewards have to bear the pressures of confrontation with management over a whole range of issues including the setting of piece rates, control over the pace of work, over safe working conditions, the allocation of overtime, and so on. In negotiations with management, a steward has to be sensitive to the feelings of membership or else face the risk of losing a credible negotiating stance and be left isolated. Shop stewards frequently find themselves in the situation of informally controlling and disciplining the workers they represent to avert needless and destructive conflicts. The pressures of anticipating and successfully dealing with these conflicts very often come on top of doing a full day's work, and many stewards feel as a matter of principle that they should not be seen to 'get an easy number'.

Management

Of course, while pressure for production is often greatest on first-line supervisors, it occurs all the way up the management hierarchy, often in the form of ever tightening production budgets, which may be impossible to fulfill, or deadlines which cannot be met.

The pressures on those in the managerial hierarchy often take the form of pressures to succeed in a very competitive system. This can mean long hours of work, much time spent on travel on company business, and a tendency to put career interests before family and other interests. Promotion can often mean destroying one's roots and friendships since it often involves moving to a different location. Many business executives, although they may have considerable control over other people's lives, frequently have very little control over their own. As one writer has said:

> 'Their organisations dominate them and move them about; tough company rules or customs tell them what to do, what to wear, what to believe in, and possibly even who to marry; their constitutional rights are violated, their privacy is invaded and their basic dignity is injured. All these things are done without the executives' full understanding of what is happening to them.'[2]

Promotion can often mean being confronted with a whole range of new responsibilities with which the manager cannot cope; lack of promotion can mean the frustration of being stuck in an unsatisfying dead-end job.

At all levels of the hierarchy there can be the constant insecurity engendered by fear of the sack. Relationships within the managerial hierarchy are often characterised by lack of mutual trust and much time spent in defending one's position and protecting one's interests.

Ancillary workers

The rigidity of bureaucratic hierarchies also affects ancillary workers and those who provide support services which are not central to the task of the organisation. Those who perform such 'peripheral' functions often find themselves completely excluded from the organisational structure of the firm or institution. This can mean that they suffer social isolation at work, often working in bad conditions, finding their jobs difficult to do because they are not properly integrated into the structure of the organisation, and for the same reasons, frequently having the frustration of having no opportunity of changing or improving their situation through promotion or advancement in the organisation.

Resistance to change

Bureaucratic hierarchies often produce tensions and conflicts because of their rigidity. Because they are organised along *vertical* lines it is very difficult to co-ordinate activities *horizontally*, that is, involving different individuals or units of the organisation at the same level in the organisation, or between individuals at different levels of the hierarchy but operating under different chains of authority. Also because they involve very clearly defined functions for each individual or unit, there is great resistance to adapting to changed circumstances. Changes in the organisation of production systems, for example, can involve major changes in the organisational system responsible for that area of production if the change is to be accomplished successfully. However, a hierarchy with a high degree of specialisation and division of function and a rigid chain of command will be resistant to such changes. When the bureaucratic hierarchy is no longer appropriate to changed circumstances, it is inevitable that individuals within the organisation will be unclear about what are the boundaries of their functions and responsibilities. They will find themselves confronted with conflicting demands which they are unable to resolve, and increasingly in dispute with their superiors and subordinates as the organisational system fails to accomplish the tasks it is set to do. Thus a surprising number of individuals at all levels in the hierarchy suffer from considerable anxiety, uncertainty, tension and conflict due to the ambiguous or contradictory demands of their jobs.

Health and the hierarchy

In this section we discuss three questions: first, is there any relationship between health and one's position in the bureaucratic hierarchy? Second, what sort of conflicts and pressures have been found to contribute to ill health and disease? Third, what ways of reacting to these conflicts and pressures also contribute to the risk of disease?

Position in the hierarchy

It is a fairly common assumption (particularly amongst managers) that the higher you rise in the hierarchy the more you will be under pressure because of greater responsibilities. Related to this is the idea that the stresses suffered by business executives and managers are a lot more severe and damaging than those suffered at the lower levels of the hierarchy. When you actually look at the evidence these ideas don't get very much support. Indeed, if there is a relationship between disease and where you are in the hierarchy, it seems just as likely that the higher you go in the hierarchy the more insulated and protected you are from the stresses and pressures that people lower down suffer. Whilst some studies have found more coronary heart disease higher in the hierarchy, others have found just the opposite and yet more have found no difference. The incidence of peptic ulcers – which is closely related to anxiety, nervous strain and feelings of inadequacy, frustration and resentment – is highest among foremen, followed in some studies by business executives. At higher levels in hierarchies there is less sickness absence for both physical and mental ailments, and a greater proportion of people tend to consider themselves in excellent health, compared to lower down the hierarchy. Thus in one study over a third of craftsmen, foremen, skilled, unskilled and miscellaneous workers said their health was poor to only fair, whereas only 3% of managers had less than excellent health.

Conflicts and hierarchies

As we saw earlier there are many sources of conflict, pressure and stress in hierarchies. There is much evidence which links repeated exposure to these stresses with coronary heart disease, with factors which have been linked to coronary heart disease like high cholesterol levels in the blood, with various neurotic complaints like tension, depression and anxiety, and with dissatisfaction with one's work and job.

Here is a list of some of the more important of these stresses. It is easy to see how they form part of the different aspects of working in hierarchies discussed earlier.

- Direct conflicts with supervisors.
- 'Role conflicts' – for example, when torn by conflicting job demands or undertaking tasks which the worker does not want to do or does not think are part of the job specification.
- 'Role ambiguity' – not knowing exactly what the work objectives are, not knowing what colleagues and supervisors expect from each worker, and being generally unclear about the scope and responsibilities of the job.
- Having too much responsibility.
- Having rigid work deadlines to meet which are very difficult to fulfill.
- Being overworked, both in the sense of having too much to do, and having work that is too difficult to do.
- Having work that involves different sectors of the organisation, and which involves continually crossing organisational boundaries.

How people behave in hierarchies

Just as some people have been found to be more susceptible to occupationally related diseases than others so people behave differently in hierarchies. Some people are ambitious, rising rapidly through the ranks of the hierarchy. They tend to be hard driving, impatient, aggressive, and hostile to others, and with a continual sense of urgency; they tend to involve themselves in a range of work activities, and are willing to take on additional responsibilities, putting themselves under considerable pressure of work and the constant stress of deadlines. This way of responding has come to be designated the 'type A' personality, in contrast to 'type B', which is altogether more calm and placid. The 'type A' personality reads like a caricature of the 'ideal executive' in a multinational corporation; however, you can see this syndrome of behaviour in many different people in a variety of jobs in many different organisations.

'Type A' people are more prone to coronary heart disease, and as we have said before, one factor that increases the risk of coronary heart disease is smoking. People who are in jobs with excessive pressure, where they are overburdened with work, and have to meet constant deadlines are very often heavy smokers. Such people are in jobs where they are forced to behave in ways characteristic of the 'type A' personality, and their recourse to smoking only multiplies their risk of coronary heart disease.

Are there any alternatives to bureaucratic hierarchies?

If hierarchies inevitably create the range of stresses and pressures we have been discussing, is there any way of avoiding these problems? A vast range of solutions have been proposed, most of them with the fundamental idea that it is desirable that workers should become more involved in, and have a greater say in, the running of the organisations in which they work, so that these organisations can in turn better represent their needs, interests and aspirations.

'Autonomous work groups'

Many schemes focus only on the lower end of the hierarchy — production workers and their immediate supervisors. The formation of 'autonomous work groups' are a good example of this: production is organised around groups of workers (often about ten to twenty) who have the responsibility for the production of a particular component, sub-assembly, or product, and who, within the group can allocate the work amongst the members as they see fit. Such groups often also take responsibility for such functions as materials supply and quality control. This eliminates the lowest levels of production management, and those levels of production management that are left are to some extent transformed from a control function to one of support. Such changes can, quite clearly, improve the quality of many production jobs and increase the control of workers over the immediate processes involved in their work.

*An example of 'new forms of work organisation' applied to an assembly line –
at the Saab–Scania engine assembly plant in Sweden.*

A conveyor line brings a supply of heavy motor parts which are then diverted into
'loops' in the line where a group of workers assembles the entire engine. With a
conventional assembly line the engine assembly takes place on the main
assembly line on which each worker does one simple job at one position on the
line.

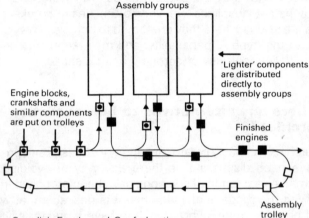

Assembly groups

Engine blocks,
crankshafts and
similar components
are put on trolleys

'Lighter' components
are distributed
directly to
assembly groups

Finished
engines

Assembly
trolley

Source: Swedish Employers' Confederation.

The advantages of the change are that the assembly groups can become more
'autonomous' or free of direct supervision, the pressure of time on the line is
decreased, and the individual can, after more training, assemble a complete
engine himself.

However the rather limited nature of such democratisation should
also be realised; thus for example, decisions over recruitment or
training policies, over investment in plant, or the design of the
machinery of production (all of which strongly affect the work of
the autonomous work group) are usually outside its powers of
decision; and this is not to mention any of the broader, financial,
planning, and other decisions that affect the overall running of the
organisation.

Involvement at all levels of the hierarchy

The problems of hierarchical organisation affect those at all levels
in the hierarchy and can only be overcome by decentralisation of
decision-making power from the top down. This decentralisation
should enable all those involved in any particular task or function of
the organisation to plan and organise their work together either

directly in 'autonomous work groups' or in planning committees made up of representatives of all the interests involved.

However, for any experiment in participation or democracy to be successful those negotiating such schemes should always remember that still the potential conflict between those who own the organisation and those who work in it will remain. Such a scheme should therefore fulfill at least the following four principles.

● It must be introduced democratically and enjoy the active support of all concerned. Participation cannot be imposed from the top, but must be built from the bottom reflecting the local interests and past experience of those involved.

● It should recognise the importance of workers' past relationships with management, and should not be an attempt to bypass traditional collective bargaining procedures or undermine trade union organisation.

● Advisory influence is not enough. The right to decide on a small number of matters is more important to workers than the right to give advice or express opinions on a large number. Such advice can always be ignored.

● The establishment of committees is not enough. Many systems of committees are just superimposed over the regular hierarchical organisation. It is necessary to change the traditional form of control of production (including planning, budgeting, management, wage systems, etc) at the same time as giving employees increased control over decisions at all levels in the organisation from section and department level up to general management and administration.

References
1 Quoted in W. F. Whyte, *Men at Work*, Dorsey, 1961.
2 H. Murrell, *Work, Stress and Mental Strain*, Work Research Unit, Department of Employment, 1978.

6 Skill, automation and the control of work

'Advances in production technology and the application of "scientific management" have led to the simplification of work in terms of both the manual and
intellectual contributions demanded of employees. This has resulted in the
creation of a great many jobs in industry which require very little skill and offer
almost no scope for workers to use their initiative, creativity or to make decisions. The situation has not come about by accident but as part of a deliberate
policy to employ unskilled labour and eliminate, as far as possible, the scope for
human error. Thus many machine operators and workers on production,
assembly and packaging lines carry out repetitive tasks, with work cycles from a
few minutes to as little as a few seconds. An additional stress is frequently
imposed in the form of mechanised pacing by conveyor belts. A concomitant of
mass production is the growth of large factories and large organisations; the
consequence is that individual workers have difficulty in understanding what is
going on, identifying with the company or relating to the people with whom they
work. An associated phenomenon is that of "bureaucratisation". That is to say
introducing systems under which those aspects of behaviour not determined by
the technology are controlled by rules and regulations from a central authority;
local discretion and initiative are again denied. Much the same philosophy has
been applied to clerical work and the provision of services in the form of
specialisation, bureaucratisation and the growth of large organisations'.[1] (Gilbert
Jessup, sometime Director of the Work Research Unit of the Department of
Employment.)

'Scientific management' and stress

This chapter is about the relationship between the design and
organisation of work, and the machinery of production systems.
The quote from Gilbert Jessup outlines the typical characteristics
of much modern industry. The increasing rationalisation of work
with each task divided into smaller and smaller elements, requiring
less and less skill to perform, has supposedly been in the interests
of greater productive efficiency. However, the need to enforce
ever higher rates of production has led to increasing discipline and
control over the labour force. In turn, workers have resisted these
increasingly inhuman conditions of work, through strikes, higher

rates of absence from work and high labour turnover. In many industries the rigid control of ever more trivial and meaningless work has become increasingly incompatible with the drive for productive efficiency, because of these effects on labour turnover, absence, and industrial relations. In the last few years solutions to this dilemma have been suggested in alternative ways of organising work which are designed to increase satisfaction with work and foster higher productivity. This chapter will also discuss some of the effects of automation on skills and stress at work, and at some of the pressures on workers who operate complex machine systems.

Working on the line

Assembly line work probably represents the ultimate system of 'scientific management' of labour. Work is organised into a series of minute and repetitive tasks, each of which is performed by a different worker. The pace at which the work is done is controlled by the speed of the line — the planning and design of work, the worker's freedom to decide how best to perform it, is taken from the worker and appropriated by management. The assembly line worker is confronted by a system which is geared to producing at an ever higher rate of production, and where the possibility of individual intelligent and creative action is removed. The worker is subjected to a level of control that is second only to that exercised over a robot or an automatic machine. For these reasons such work has been described as 'dehumanised'.

However, no system of control is absolute, and there is always the possibility of resistance to even the most tightly controlled and authoritarian system of work organisation. Thus what actually happens on the shop floor is the outcome of the pattern of resistance and accommodation between management and workers and their representatives on a collective level. On an individual level each worker makes the best accommodation that he or she can to the pressures and demands of working on the line.

Fragmentation of skills

In the car industry, with the speed of the line being anything up to sixty cars an hour, each sequence of work operations can average about one minute. Each job typically comprises two or three short operations, repeated incessantly day after day. The work has few skill requirements and requires little or no training. Most of the jobs can be learnt in a few hours, and to become proficient takes no more than a few days.

Speed-up

Perhaps the worst aspect of working on the line is the unrelenting pressure of the line coming at the worker all the time. The determination of the speed of the line is a major source of conflict and dispute between workers, their shop floor representatives and management. In the car industry this has centred around the prevention of 'speed-up' – the systematic increase in the pace of production, often by gradually increasing the speed of the line during a shift. Thus the right for a shop steward to have a key to the switch that controls the speed of the line has been a hard won right guaranteeing that the speed of the line is negotiable between unions and management. However, even with mutually agreed line speeds, the very nature of assembly line work allows only the minimum of work control to be exercised by workers.

Unvarying pace

The consistent and unvarying pace of the line takes no account of fluctuations in mood or feelings of fatigue. Many workers find the unvarying speed of the line far more oppressive than the actual speed itself. In some jobs it is possible by working fast to build up a 'bank' of completed operations, which allows a few minutes break. Some workers try 'doubling up' – working furiously at two jobs for an hour while a mate takes a rest and then switching over. However, the harder they work to create more time, the more management will try to take it away by tightening up on production standards.

We explained in the chapter on shiftwork that many of our bodily functions vary rhythmically throughout the 24 hour cycle of the day (this includes heart rate, body temperature and the production of certain hormones). When we determine our own pace of work we tend to vary it to accommodate this bodily rhythm. Thus it is no wonder that workers find intense, unchanging, machine-paced pressure of work oppressive.

Freedom of movement

Working on assembly lines is monotonous, repetitive and intensely paced, and there is no escape from it. A simple thing like going to the toilet means having to get someone to replace you on the line. It is impossible to stop for a few minutes.

What are the effects of working on the line?

Fatigue

In one study of assembly line workers in the car industry half the workers complained that the excessive pressure of the line caused fatigue and exhaustion at the end of the day. Older workers are less able to cope and there is a sharp fall-off in the proportion of men and women working on assembly lines over the age of 40.[3] It is often said that after 10 years on the assembly line workers are burnt out and it is frequently management policy to recruit only younger workers who can take the pressure.

Quality of work

The intense pace of the line also means that the quality of work suffers. Many workers find it a considerable source of frustration that they cannot do the job as well as they would wish. Quality of work was a central issue in the strike by General Motors workers at the Lordstown plant in the USA in the early 1970s where the ruthless cutting back of the workforce and intense pace of the line made it impossible to guarantee the production of safe vehicles.

Social isolation

Although on many assembly lines workers are close enough to exchange the odd comment or joke these social contacts tend to be extremely superficial. The assembly line demands nearly all the worker's attention and concentration because of the speed of the line and the detailed nature of the work; the high levels of noise in many plants makes it very difficult to be heard and understood; and social contacts tend to be restricted to those working in the immediate vicinity. Thus, assembly line work tends to prevent the worker from deriving any social satisfaction from work. The noise, it should be added, is yet another source of tension and strain.

In short, almost every source of human satisfaction has been designed out in the interests of greater control over the workforce and ever higher levels of production. The only rational attitude becomes one of pure instrumentality – 'I'm only here for the money'.

'You don't achieve anything here. A robot could do it. The line here is made for morons. It doesn't need any thought. They tell you that. "We don't pay you for thinking" they say. Everyone comes to realize that they're not doing a worthwhile job. They're just on the line. For the money. Nobody likes to think that they're a failure. Its bad when you know that you're just a little cog. You just look at your pay packet – you look at what it does for your wife and kids. That's the answer.'[2]

High labour turnover is common in assembly line production. But there are many workers who get trapped on the line. The relatively high wages in the car industry may enable workers to take out a mortgage and buy a house, and with a family to maintain the financial insecurity of giving up a high-wage job cannot be risked. Such pressures force workers to try to adapt rather than to quit. Financial commitments bind workers to their employers. Such firms operate a points system where an individual has a greater chance of a job if he or she is married, has children and holds a mortgage. Such workers will be less likely to leave, to be absent, to go on strike, and will want to take any overtime that they can get.

Automation, skills, control of work and employment

The 'rationalisation' of work into simple and repetitive elements often occurs at the same time as the mechanisation of production. Assembly lines are the classic example of this; but many other jobs which involve working with production machinery have the same characteristics – skills are fragmented into smaller and smaller elements and intense pace of work is enforced either by the speed of the machinery itself, by rigid discipline, or by very tight piece rates. It is often claimed that one solution to this gradual 'de-skilling' of work is further automation – to get machines to do jobs that have become so simple and repetitive that they are 'machine-like'. This, it is argued, would release workers to do more skillful, interesting and challenging jobs operating the more complex machines which control the automatic processes.

Unfortunately, it is not as simple as this. Automation can affect the skill content of jobs in many different ways and the effects on skills will in turn influence the satisfaction a worker can get from the job. Also, it is one of the deliberate effects of automation to eliminate as many jobs as possible.

Automation can replace deskilled jobs. Robots and automatic welding machines are increasingly used in car assembly, replacing jobs that were previously done manually.

Automation can directly deskill jobs. Numerically controlled machine tools are a particularly good example of this, where the skills of the machinist has been, as it were, incorporated into the machine, whose precise and complex movements have been preprogrammed, reducing the skilled machinist to the level of a machine minder. Another example concerns the job of maintenance workers in increasingly complex automatic systems. As the machinery becomes more complex and sophisticated, automatic fault diagnosis becomes more feasible and necessary, and slot-in disposable replacement components are used increasingly. Thus the skilled job of fault diagnosis and repair becomes one of routinely slotting in replacement parts. Even the highly complex intellectual skills of workers like draughtsmen and computer programmers become more controlled and fragmented and hence more subject to rigid discipline through the process of routinising and automating more and more functions.

Automation changes the distribution of skills required in the production process. Typically there is a large reduction in the number of skilled production workers, a small increase in highly skilled jobs such as programmers and maintenance technicians, and a large increase in the proportion of unskilled workers. Figure 7 shows how this changed pattern of skills has affected the textile industry.

Automation can create a new pattern of stresses on the worker. In continuous process industries, like chemicals, where the whole process of production is automated, the major functions are maintenance and monitoring of these automatic processes. Such jobs, although routine and often monotonous for much of the time, confer some degree of freedom in organising work, involve a greater sense of responsibility for the production process, and stimulate greater social involvement in work because of the interdependence of different functions.

However, jobs monitoring or controlling the operation of automated plant are themselves subject to the pressure to increase productivity by reducing manning levels. This leads to a decline in the importance of team work in the organisation of work and operators find themselves increasingly working in isolation. This can be a problem not only because of the loneliness and isolation

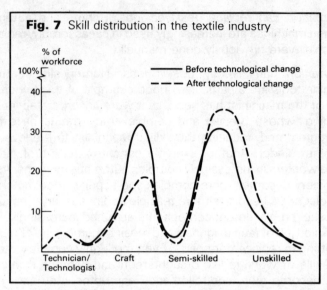

Fig. 7 Skill distribution in the textile industry

Source: 'The economic and employment aspects of technological change' – John Wyte in *Technology, Choice and the Future of Work*, BA Symposium, 22.11.78

itself, but also because of the anxiety of operators about their responsibilities and the possibility that a critical emergency might lead an operator to panic. One operator described it like this:

'Fifteen foot by nine. That constant hum. The darkness outside. No-one. No one there at all. All that responsibility. You don't know what's going on outside. It got me. Is it really going right? It worries you.'[4]

Automation can increase management control over the production process, and restrict the control of workers over their jobs. This is certainly true of numerically controlled machine tools, and of any other piece of automatic equipment which permits the quantity of work to be logged up as it is done. A rather extreme example illustrates how automated systems can be used to control the movements and activities of office workers. A large insurance company in Paris installed a computer which controlled staff movements in the following way. Glass partitions were installed controlling access to each floor; the doors in the partitions could only be opened by inserting a special plastic card. Each insertion of the card was monitored by the computer and thus a check was kept on the movements of all those working in the office.

Automation can lead to an increase in shiftworking. This is because automation is costly and there is thus pressure to keep automated plant going continuously.

Automation can lead to a reduction in employment. Up until now the main effects of mechanisation and automation have been in job losses, firstly in agriculture and mining and secondly in manufacturing and construction. In Britain, between June 1975 and June 1976, 653,500 jobs were lost in manufacturing, construction and the utilities. There has been a similar pattern of job losses throughout Europe and this process has come to be called 'de-industrialisation'. Although many job-losses have been caused by changes in demand and competition, technological changes have meant a reduction in the number of production workers in industry compared with the number of clerical and administrative workers. But a major threat to employment in the future comes from the new micro-electronic technology which will have the worst effects on clerical and administrative workers (essentially any worker who handles information). ASTMS, a major white collar union, has estimated that by 1985 the number of information workers in the economy will have reached 50% of the total workforce and will be of a similar proportion in 1991. The potential for job loss is thus vast. It is also unlikely that there will be any expansion in any other employment sector – the opposite is more likely. Therefore a huge increase in unemployment is predicted.

Automation can affect the design of work in offices. Automatic data-processing systems are designed to centralise and to integrate all relevant functions like computing, constructing files, storage and retrieval, updating, correcting etc. The most common form of office automation is the visual display unit (VDU) – a television screen which displays the information being entered into or extracted from the computer. All the various functions mentioned above can be done on one VDU, thus eliminating all the time spent walking around the office filing area, sorting through files, waiting, and talking with other staff whilst doing this work. It is possible to automatically monitor the operation of each machine to ensure effectively their most efficient and constant usage. The consequences of this can be an increased pressure of work and a marked reduction in the social content of any such work.

Centralised automatic office systems have great potential for increasing the range of functions and tasks that can easily be performed by any one worker – potentially increasing interest and satisfaction with work. But this is only possible if the VDU operator retains some control over the planning, organisation, selection and use of the information that he or she is handling.

However, there is the danger that in most cases the VDU operator's job will be one of routinely typing in and extracting standard information in a highly repetitive manner, while the use and control over that information is reserved to a higher level in the hierarchy. This is particularly dangerous because the VDU operator will be tied to the machine for a large proportion of the working day — which is known to cause eyestrain and fatigue. The only way to avoid this fatigue and eyestrain is to have regular and frequent breaks. This should be combined with increasing the range of activities performed by each operator thus increasing the social contact and the skill content of the job.

In summary, therefore, the crucial aspects of automation or the introduction of any new technical system to work are the effects this will have on the skills and range of activities involved in any job, and the amount of control each worker has over their process of work. The first aspect will affect the interest and satisfaction a worker has with his or her work which will in turn be associated with the worker's mental health. The second aspect will be reflected in the amount of pressure and strain the worker feels, which may be shown in symptoms of fatigue and anxiety.

Complex machine systems and stress

Many workers who operate complex machine systems have to make repeated, urgent, difficult and dangerous decisions often involving safety risks, when the consequences of failure could be disastrous. Many of these jobs are in the transport industry. They include those who pilot or drive ships, planes, buses, trucks, etc., and those who direct and organise the traffic (air traffic controllers, train dispatchers and signalmen for example).

In pre-automation days, train dispatchers in the United States were asked to make approximately five decisions a minute over an eight hour day, six days a week. Each of these decisions involved life or death for the train passengers or crews. Air traffic controllers have a similar job which is highly complex and carries heavy personal responsibility. It is particularly difficult during periods of high traffic density, during critical incidents and on the frequent occasions when it is difficult to communicate to the pilots. Ship pilots have to manoeuvre large and unwieldy vessels around confined spaces, often in foul weather, day or night, working from an unfamiliar bridge. Air pilots, and truck, bus and taxi drivers are all confronted with recurrent, complex instant decisions to make under conditions of responsibility and danger, the differences being only the size and complexity of their machines and their mode of travel.

These jobs often have an intense pace and pressure of work which is largely outside the control of the operator. Thus they are liable to cause feelings of tension, fatigue and anxiety. There are, therefore, two main ways in which these pressures could be alleviated. Firstly, the level of manning and the pattern of responsibility should prevent the overloading of any one operator. Secondly, the organisation of work schedules should ensure sufficient time for good rest and recuperation between work shifts as well as adequate rest breaks within shifts, so that the operator is feeling and functioning at his or her best throughout the whole working period.

Pressure of work and health

Symptoms of strain

There have been many studies of the effect of the jobs described in this chapter. Not surprisingly, workers in these jobs frequently feel themselves to be under stress. The table shows some of the features of work which are most often found to be stressful, and some of the more important symptoms of strain which result from these features.

Table 5 Stresses of work and related symptoms of strain

Aspects of work	Symptoms of strain
work which is repetitive and requires no skill	hormonal symptoms of the 'emergency response'
lack of control over work methods and pace	cardiovascular strain – increased heart rate and blood pressure
restricted movement and social interaction	feelings of strain and tension
work in high levels of noise	fatigue
dangerous work	anxiety
work involving quick decisions and high levels of responsibility	difficulty in relaxing after work
work of intense pace with no opportunity to rest	disturbances of sleep
	digestive disturbances
	depressed mood

Physical health

A number of studies have shown higher levels of stress-related diseases in occupations in which workers suffer the stresses outlined in this chapter. Higher levels of coronary heart disease have been found amongst air pilots, some bus and taxi drivers, train dispatchers and assembly line workers. A high incidence of hypertension has been found amongst train drivers and air traffic controllers; and a higher incidence of peptic ulcers and diabetes has also been found in some studies of air traffic controllers.

Psychological disorders

Jobs which are monotonous, highly controlled and which impose considerable work pressure have been associated with a higher incidence of neuroses (insomnia, anxiety and depression are typical reactions – see Chapter 2). Typical jobs of this type are machine-paced assembly line work, jobs which are highly repetitive, and jobs which require constant attention, particularly where there is little scope for initiative or responsibility.

Industrial hysteria

There is one fairly unusual phenomenon which can affect large numbers of workers simultaneously. It is called 'industrial hysteria'. There are a whole variety of symptoms associated with industrial hysteria, but they typically include laboured breathing, dizziness, nausea, fainting, headaches and general feelings of malaise amongst a large section of the workforce. There is usually a 'trigger' which precipitates the hysteria, but this precipitating factor cannot explain the symptoms. The cause of the 'hysteria' is the strain, anxiety and tension engendered by the work environment. Characteristic situations in which the hysteria occurs are where workers are performing monotonous and repetitive jobs in hazardous working conditions (for example, extremes of temperature, noise, or fumes). Factors which contribute to the hysteria are a hostile relationship between management and workers, and genuine fear and anxiety amongst the workers about their health and safety.

One example of industrial hysteria occurred in a shoe factory where a malfunctioning air-conditioning unit caused a build up of fumes from the glue used to assemble shoes. The glue fumes were not toxic but three or four workers at a time began fainting. Police or ambulances were sometimes called, and it happened again and again over a period of several weeks. Management responded by removing the pay-phone from the plant – the workers struck for six days until the phones were replaced; management then sacked eight shop stewards. The following day workers again fainted, police and ambulances were called as more and more workers fell ill. In all 70 workers fell ill. 48 were taken to hospital but, in fact, none were admitted. The fumes, by themselves, were not toxic enough to make anyone faint.

Far more serious reactions can be prompted occasionally by intolerable working conditions, particularly among susceptible workers. In one case in the United States an assembly line worker shot two foremen and a toolsetter. In recording a verdict of manslaughter due to temporary insanity the judge took into account the 'abominable' conditions in which the man had been working. In another case the Supreme Court of the State of Michigan awarded compensation against General Motors, for a man whose schizophrenic psychosis was brought on by the pressure of his job.

Mental health

A definite relationship has been consistently found between the characteristics of a job in terms of its skill, complexity and interest, and the worker's mental health. Workers who find their work monotonous and uninteresting, who feel they have no control over their work, who suffer from mental stress from the pressure of work and who suffer from social isolation at work, tend to have much lower levels of mental health.

One study of car workers found that only 10% of young workers performing repetitive semi-skilled jobs could be considered to have a high level of mental health. When jobs paced by machine were considered by themselves this figure fell to 7%.

Mental health is also affected by how high expectations or aspirations are. The lower such aspirations are, the easier it is to adapt to them. But this confronts unskilled or semi-skilled workers with depressing options: either they maintain relatively high expectations, which will lead to constant frustration, or they limit their expectations, which will lead to a drab and meaningless existence.

Alcohol and drugs

Many workers turn to alcohol and other drugs as a way of coping with the frustration of their work (though, of course, this is not the only reason why people drink or take drugs). Many find it necessary to drink large quantities of alcohol during their lunch breaks to enable them to stand the pressure of overwhelming boredom of their jobs. Others turn to psychotropic drugs. In one car plant in the United States 15% of the 3,400 workforce were estimated to be addicted to heroin.

Is there any solution to the 'dehumanisation' of work?

The question is – is it possible to consider not only the technological elements of production, but how workers' social and psychological needs interact with the technology? In recent years much consideration has been given to 'new forms of work organisation', which, its advocates claim, can resolve the contradictions between the demands for productive efficiency and the needs of workers for socially and psychologically satisfying work.

'New forms of work organisation'

It is difficult to give a precise definition to the phrase 'new forms of work organisation' because there is no single 'recipe' which can make a job satisfying, or any 'off-the-shelf' package which can be applied to every job. The emphasis of this approach to job design is that every job has to be approached differently because every job requires its own unique solution. Whilst on the one hand, there are certain technical requirements of production – certain processes have to be gone through to produce the required product – on the other hand, there are the needs and interests of the workers in that organisation. It is argued that it is possible to achieve an optimum compromise between the two aspects of the system. While there is no 'recipe' there are certain principles which should form the basis of job design. A brief summary of some of these follows:

- Each job should contain a variety of different tasks (to prevent boredom and fatigue); ideally these tasks should be co-ordinated so that the worker can select the method of working he or she prefers, and can relate his or her work to that of others. The resulting work cycle should be of an optimum length so that a rhythm of work can be maintained. Too short a cycle means too much stopping and starting; too long a cycle makes it difficult to build up a rhythm of work.
- Workers should have some scope for setting their own

standards of quantity and quality of production, and should get some feedback about how they are performing.

- Each job should include tasks that require some degree of care, skill, knowledge or effort that is worthy of respect, and each job should contribute to making a useful product.
- Where possible, jobs should be organised around group-working rather than individual working. Thus different jobs should be interlocking or interdependent, or be rotated amongst the members of the group, or at least workers should be in the same area of work space. This should increase mutual co-operation and understanding, ameliorate the effects of stress, and make the work of the group as a whole appear more 'meaningful'.

In short, each job should involve some kind of socially recognised skill, and each worker should form part of a well integrated social unit.

It is often suggested that workers should also participate in decisions that affect the content and organisation of their work. Such changes would imply a reduction of direct supervision and greater freedom from management control.

'New forms of work organisation' in practice

These principles are general and abstract, but how do they work in practice? To date trade unions in Britain have rarely campaigned for new forms of work organisation. Thus the impetus for change often comes from management. Without being too cynical, it is important to consider why there should be an increased interest by management in the quality of working life. In general terms, managements are concerned with their current industrial relations problems, rates of absence and labour turnover, productivity and profitability, and perhaps with trying to foster a sense of loyalty to the company amongst its employees. Fostering increased satisfaction with work can be seen as one way of enhancing these aims. Another is by promoting ideas of job flexibility and multi-skilling (as a process of job enrichment) which can be used to eliminate so-called 'restrictive practices' which protect workers from excessive management demands and provide unions with flexibility in the collective bargaining process. Thus two of the most important consequences of a reorganisation of work methods may be:

- A reduction in the number of jobs available (although this may not mean redundancies – but a process of 'natural wastage').
- In the long term, an undermining of the independence and bargaining strength of the union, through assimilating shop stewards into the management decision-making apparatus without releasing real control over these decisions.

For these reasons it is important to appreciate what any proposed new scheme of work organisation may involve. New forms of work organisation *can* improve jobs. However many so-called job-enrichment and participation schemes are cosmetic exercises designed to 'solve an industrial relations problem' on the cheap. Changes in job content and in the 'style' of management are no *substitute* for real improvements in wages, in the physical conditions of work, or in security of employment. Also, any real control or influence over the way work is organised involves having a real say in the decisions which affect the way things are done at the point of production. Such matters include payment systems, organisational structure, training, support services, changes in technology, as well as questions of autonomy and discretion on the job, task variety, and group organisation.

Considering new forms of work organisation in this broad way can give new scope to unions to extend the areas of collective bargaining. The application of new forms of work organisation conclusively demonstrates that there is nothing inevitable, or technologically-determined, about the way work has been traditionally organised into a rigid hierarchy, an ever-increasing fragmentation of tasks, and an oppressive system of supervision and control.

References
1 Gilbert Jessup, Director of the Work Research Unit, Department of the Employment in *Technology as if people mattered*, WRU Occasional paper no. 12.
2 Quoted in H. Beynon, *Working for Ford*, Penguin, 1975.
3 R. Blauner, *Alienation and Freedom*, University of Chicago Press, 1964.
4 Quoted in T. Nichols and P. Armstrong, *Workers Divided*, Fontana, 1976.
5 A. Kornhauser, *Mental Health of the Industrial Worker*, Wiley, 1965.

7 Trade union action

Utopian aims?

Is it utopian for workers and their trade unions to demand the right to work and security of employment? Is it utopian to insist that workers be paid to meet their needs and paid according to a system that respects their dignity and integrity as workers? Is it utopian that workers insist upon hours of work which are compatible with their biological and social well-being, and that their work stimulates their creativity and develops their skills without overtaxing their physical and mental resources? It is too much to ask that workers be given the right to participate fully in the social organisation of their work without being subject to arbitrary authority?

It might be said these *are* utopian aims, but, in fact, as this book has shown, the absence of any of these general conditions constitutes a potential threat to the workers' well-being and health.

Achieving a psychologically and socially healthy working environment has not generally been a priority objective of the trade union movement. Of course many of the issues discussed in this book are crucial areas of negotiation – rates of pay, overtime and shift bonuses, productivity deals, and the organisation of shift systems. But the link between these questions and stress has rarely been made. Furthermore, many other sources of stress, such as repetitive and monotonous work, controlled and paced by machinery, are accepted as normal and inevitable features of working life.

How can the issue of stress at work be firmly placed on the agenda for trade union negotiations?

Getting 'stress at work' to the bargaining table

Those who are involved in negotiating working conditions should both take account of factors which affect the 'quality of working life' in *present* areas of collective bargaining, and should also extend the scope of collective bargaining to include *all* factors that affect the determination of working conditions.

- Wage bargaining should attempt to reduce reliance on overtime and shift bonuses by boosting basic rates proportionately more than bonuses and overtime rates.
- Incentive payment systems should be seen to be fair to all those who work them, and should incorporate some protection against the relentless pressure to intensify the pace of work.
- Job grading systems which discriminate against a particular group of workers (such as women) and which institutionalise sectors of inadequate pay must be resisted.

However, many areas of work stress fall outside the normal scope of collective bargaining and require getting involved in work systems and work organisation at the planning stage. It may be possible to work out a shift system that reduces the number of workers required on the night shift, and which maximises the number of free weekends available to each shiftworker; it might even be possible to avoid shiftworking altogether. But unless trade unions are involved in the planning of production systems they will be subject to the consequences of decisions which rarely take into account the interests of those who have to man these systems. The same principle also applies to the design of jobs with the introduction of new plant and machinery. The design of a new technical system will inevitably determine to a considerable extent the content of jobs and the organisation of work. Unless workers have a voice in the design stage new systems will be designed according to technical and economic criteria alone, with little thought given to the human consequences of these decisions.

Trade union goals

Let us look in a little more detail at some of the ways in which trade unionists can counter the stresses at work.

Low pay

There is probably no single simple solution to the problem of low pay. Low paying industries are often those which have a number of features making union organisation difficult – like having a moving or seasonal workforce which works in small units (like in hotels or shops), and in which there are a high proportion of women workers and casual workers. The collective bargaining strength of any particular group of workers in these areas tends not to be very great. However dramatic gains *can* be made by collective action. This was demonstrated by the London night cleaners who joined the TGWU and formed the Cleaners Action Group which enabled them to organise effective action to improve their conditions. May Hobbs of the Cleaners Action Group describes the effect of one strike in 1971: 'The strike lasted for three weeks. We raised wages from £12 plus the 50p a week bonus for working a 45 hour week without being late, to £17.50 per week. We gained union recognition, three weeks sick pay, two weeks holiday pay and they met us on the demand for more cleaners on the building.' This is a good example of how wages can be raised if workers organise and act collectively.

On a broader front it is important that the trade union movement demands that there should be some primary level of basic pay below which no worker should fall. Equal pay legislation also needs to be more effectively implemented; this has been limited in its effects because so many women work in 'women-only' occupations where there is no obvious comparison with an equivalent men's rate. The legislation needs to be extended to include the principle of 'equal pay for work of equal value'.

Incentive payment systems

Three general principles should govern union attitudes to incentive payment systems. Firstly, such systems should be outlawed in any dangerous work situation. This would reduce the risk of accidents and avoid the anxiety of workers having to balance their safety against the amount they earn. Secondly, there should be mutuality between workers and management in the setting of performance standards. This should ensure that the standards set are seen to be fair. And thirdly, it is important for workers not to sell too much of their so-called 'unproductive' time for higher rates of pay – this would include rest-breaks, cleaning up time, time for setting up the job, etc. A certain amount of flexibility in job times is important to prevent excessive pressure of work building up.

Shiftwork

The best time to get a better deal in negotiating over shiftwork is when a shift system is about to be introduced. A government survey showed that most shift systems are introduced with little or no attempt by management to calculate the economic effects never mind the effects on workers' health.[1] It is therefore vital to insist that management justify the introduction (or continuation) of a shift system not only in economic terms, but also taking account of its effects on health and the disruption of personal, domestic and social life of those involved.

If a shift system is introduced it may be possible to minimise its effects by promoting the following principles. Wherever possible production should be transferred to the day shift so that fewer workers are involved in evening, night and early morning shifts. There should be a right of transfer to equivalent work (or early retirement for older workers) for all workers who find it difficult to adapt to shiftwork. This will go some way in preventing workers becoming trapped in shiftwork. Any shift system should guarantee adequate time for rest and leisure – this means shortening the working hours of shiftworkers, and providing frequent free weekends. Finally, the shift system should be designed to suit the special needs of those who work it.

There are many different types of shift system, and they have different disadvantages, and as Chapter 4 has shown, different aspects of shiftwork can be subject to negotiation. Although the shift system that is produced at the end of negotiations might not look the neatest on paper, it should be the best one possible for those who have to work it.

Hierarchies

It is often easier in small organisations to try out alternatives to the strict specialisation and rigid authority structure that characterise most work organisations. Successful experiments along these lines have taken place in organisations as diverse as small worker co-operatives and merchant ships. In larger organisations schemes of this type have tended to focus on the lower levels of the hierarchy – production workers and their immediate supervisors. The formation of 'autonomous work groups' (discussed in Chapter 5) are a good example of this. Such changes can, quite clearly, improve the quality of many production jobs and increase the control of workers over the immediate process involved in their work.

Two points need to be made about such schemes: first, they

frequently involve workers having to give up established practices such as job demarcation in favour of a policy of flexible and multiple skills. In making such sacrifices trade unionists need to be sure that they are getting in return a real measure of control over the process and organisation of work. Secondly, these schemes give workers no control over decisions taken higher up the management hierarchy which strongly affect the work of the 'autonomous work group' (such decisions would cover, for example, recruitment and training, investment in plant and the design of machinery).

The rationalisation of work

Chapter 6 discussed some of the principles of new forms of work organisation which are designed to reverse the dehumanising trend of 'scientific management'. Such issues are on the agenda for negotiation in industry in Scandinavia as the following framework agreement shows. The aim of job re-design was formulated in six so-called 'psychological' job demands.

Norwegian Federation of Trade Unions (LO) and the Norwegian Employers' Association (NAF) Agreement on new forms of work organisation; key headings
1. Variation and meaning in the job
2. Continuous learning on the job
3. Participation in decision-making
4. Mutual help and support for fellow workers
5. Meaningful relation between the job and social life outside
6. A desirable future in the job – not only through promotion

---

The Health and Safety at Work Act and stress

There is little legislative 'control' of the stresses at work with the exception of the protective legislation covering the employment of women and young people. However, information from the employer on matters relating to stress may be gained from thoughtful use of the 1974 Health and Safety at Work Act.

Employers have legal duties under Section 2(2)(c) of the Health and Safety at Work Act to provide:

'such *information*, instruction, training and supervision as is necessary to ensure so far as is reasonably practicable the health and safety at work of his employees'.

Regulation 7(2) of the Safety Representatives Regulations states:

'An employer shall make available to safety representatives the information within the employers knowledge, necessary to enable them to fulfil their functions . . .'

and the back-up Code of Practice defines this information as:

'6(b) information of a technical nature about hazards to health and safety and precautions deemed necessary to eliminate or minimise them.'

and 6(d):

'. . . including the results of any measurements taken by the employer or persons acting on his behalf . . .'

Thus the employer should provide information, and it is important that workers use the provisions of this act in the struggle against psychological and social stresses at work.

However, the Health and Safety at Work Act and Regulations do not constitute a perfect instrument. Information is often limited, and is frequently not objective. Scientific information is not always impartial and does not always take everything into account; therefore when it does not coincide with the experience and common sense judgement of workers it is right to be sceptical. It is frequently a good idea to seek a second, independent, opinion. However in the final analysis it is the collective experience of workers and the effectiveness of their trade union organisation which counts in ensuring change.

There are two more problems with legislation like the Health and Safety at Work Act. Firstly, information on its own is not enough, and there are no provisions for enforcement of improvements in the working environment relating to stress. Secondly, there are no standards or guidelines upon which to base any such enforcements.

A safe working level?

The usual (but by no means acceptable) process of establishing so-called 'safe' levels of exposure to hazards cannot be applied to psychological and social stresses at work.

The best that can be done is to formulate a set of guidelines like those in the Norwegian agreement referred to above. Sometimes it is possible to specify minimum standards for the design and organisation of work, but these are by no means 'safe' working limits but merely a basis upon which a process of improvement of working conditions can be started.

The way in which different psychological and social factors interact with each other at work makes it difficult to establish a clear cut chain of causation between the stresses of work and the strain and long term effects on health and well-being that result in any particular situation. As we have seen earlier, a whole range of factors affect the way workers respond to stress, and a whole range of stresses are frequently present in the same environment. This makes monitoring the work environment even more difficult.

Stress and legislation

The Scandinavian countries, Norway and Sweden, lead the way in legislating for a more psychologically and socially healthy environment and show how legislation could help tackle stress at work. Their legislation recognises that the most significant improvements in the working environment come in places where the workers directly affected are most active in initiating and creating pressure for such changes. It is also, of course, necessary that management be both willing to change, and that the organisation has sufficient power over its technical and organisational resources to effect the necessary changes. For these reasons the legislation has increased the powers of workers to define and control their working situation by guaranteeing rights to information and negotiation, through shop stewards or safety representatives, concerning all matters affecting their working environment. To get around the difficulty of specifying the certain causes of particular problems, *all* possible contributing factors are specified as relevant causes, and the workers themselves take part in deciding the order of priority in attacking the list of possible causes. And, although in certain aspects of work organisation minimum standards can be set, the emphasis of the legislation is to set the *conditions* for continuous improvement in the working environment.

This legislation provides a model which could with advantage be emulated in Britain and in other countries.

Trade unions and control of the working environment

We have argued that the elimination of the stresses of work discussed in this book depend upon workers having more say in the control of their working environment. Some managements are enlightened and see the mutual advantages that can be gained from experiments in this area. But too often programmes to increase participation in decision-making by workers fail because they are instituted by management as a last ditch attempt to solve an industrial relations problem. It is not surprising that such experiments fail, because they are undertaken in situations of mutual antagonism and mistrust, and where workers are being asked to make substantial sacrifices for what are often rather intangible benefits. *Proposals to improve the psychological and social working environment are no substitute for other trade union goals, nor should they be seen as a panacea for industrial relations problems. They are important in their own right.*

References
1 *Hours of Work, Overtime and Shiftwork*, National Board for Prices and Incomes, HMSO, 1970.

Further reading

The best general survey of research evidence on work stresses is *Work, stress and mental strain*, by Hywell Murrell, available free from the Work Research Unit (Department of Employment), Steel House, 11 Tothill St, London SW1H 9LN. *Stress* by T. Cox (Macmillan 1978) is a more detailed study of the mechanisms of stress both at work and elsewhere.

A very good book on women and work includes a separate chapter on work stress and health. It is *Women's work, women's health* by Jeanne Mager Stellman, Pantheon Books, New York (1977).

The most up to date account of low pay in Britain is an article by Chris Pond called 'Low Pay' in *Labour and Equality* edited by N. Bosanquet and P. Townsend, Heinemann (1980).

The TUC booklet *Overtime and shiftworking* contains some good points for negotiating over these two issues. Available from the TUC, Great Russell St, London WC1.

There are two useful books on payment systems and work study in the Trade Union Industrial Studies series from Arrow Books. They are *Pay at Work* by Bill Conboy and *Work Study* by Jim Powell.

A good evaluation of the evidence on shiftwork is *Nightwork* by J. Carpentier and P. Cazamain, published by the International Labour Office, Geneva. Available from the ILO, New Bond St, London W1Y 9LA.

The Shop Steward's Guide to Work Organisation points out some of the problems and dangers of new forms of work organisation. It is published by Spokesman Books, Bertrand Russell House, Gamble St, Nottingham NG7 4ET. *New Forms of Work Organisation* by L. Klein is a more detailed study published by Cambridge University Press (1976).

Glossary

Acute Referring to a disorder or complaint with a sudden outset and short duration. See chronic.

Angina pectoris A type of chest pain due to lack of oxygen supplied to the heart muscle.

Anxiety Generalized feeling of fear and apprehension.

Apathy Absence of feeling or emotion; indifference.

Autonomy Freedom from external control.

Biological rhythm Periodic fluctuation of physiological activity, as over the 24 hour period.

Caffeine Stimulant substance in coffee.

Cardiovascular system The blood circulation system including the heart and blood vessels (veins and arteries).

Cholesterol A waxy material widely distributed throughout the body.

Chronic Referring to a relatively permanent disorder or complaint.

Coronary artery disease A disorder characterised by thickening of the coronary arteries.

Coronary heart disease A disorder produced by coronary artery disease and manifest in angina pectoris and coronary thrombosis.

Coronary thrombosis 'Heart attack' due to a clot forming in and blocking a coronary artery.

Depression Emotional state marked by great sadness and apprehension, feelings of worthlessness and guilt, withdrawal from others, loss of sleep, appetite and sexual desire, and either lethargy or agitation.

Exhaustion Extreme fatigue.

Fatigue Feeling of limpness and bodily discomfort often due to excessive work or other activity, and characterised by an aversion to continued activity.

Frustration Thwarting of a mood or a desire.

Gastric Connected with the stomach, e.g. gastric ulcer.

Hormones Chemical released by the endocrine glands that regulates activity in various bodily organs.

Hypertension High blood pressure.

Individual susceptibility Concerns the idea that different individuals are affected differently by stress or other factors.

Insecurity Uncertainty, lacking confidence.

Insomnia Chronic sleeplessness.

Irritability Being easily annoyed or excited to anger.

Lethargy Morbid drowsiness.

Listlessness Lack of interest and desire, indifference and inactivity.

Measured day work (MDW) A system in which pay is fixed against some specified level of performance. The system depends on job evaluation to fix the level of pay, and on work measurement to set the performance level required and to monitor the actual level achieved.

Mental health A characterisation of a general attitude to oneself, one's social situation (including work) and to life in general.

Nervous disorder A neurotic or psychosomatic disturbance.

Neurosis Emotional disturbance often characterised by anxiety, which is sufficiently severe to begin to disturb one's social and emotional life.

'Night worker's neurosis' A term which has been used by some authorities to describe the pattern of fatigue and anxiety leading to depression or aggression, which is experienced by some shiftworkers.

Payment by results (PBR) A system in which payment varies according to output, thus providing an incentive to produce more. It includes both piecework where payment is by the piece or unit of work, and bonus and premium systems in which a basic time wage is supplemented by the bonus or premium which depends on output.

Peptic ulcer Open sore in lining of the stomach or duodenum.

Psychological To do with the phenomena of conscious life and behaviour.

Psychosis Severe personality disorder involving loss of contact with reality, often with delusions and hallucinations. Usually requires hospitalisation.

Psychosomatic Referring to physical symptoms and disorders which result from continued emotional mobilisation under stress.

Psychotropic drug A drug which affects one's mental state.

Rotation direction The sequence of shifts in a three or four shift system. A regular rotation direction follows the sequence: morning, afternoon, night; an inverse rotation would be morning, night, afternoon.

Rotation period The number of consecutive days on the same shift. A short rotation period would be less than seven days; a long period greater than seven days.

Scientific management The systematic division of work into smaller and smaller elements which are placed under rigid supervision and control by management.

Shiftwork A system in which the working period (or shift) occurs at least partly outside the normal working day. Shift systems can either be permanent, alternating, or rotating.

Sleep debt An accumulated sleep loss due to inadequate sleep on succeeding nights.

Social death A term which has been used to describe the extreme social isolation experienced by some shiftworkers.

Strain The effects of stress on the individual. Strain is shown in changes in mood and feelings, changes in physiological reactions, and in behaviour and interpersonal relations.

Stress Any demand or threat which requires coping behaviour.

Stroke Blockage or rupture of large blood vessel in the brain leading to impairment of brain function.

Symptom An observable manifestation of a physical or mental disorder.

Syndrome Group or pattern of symptoms which occur together in a disorder.

Tension Feeling of strain, uneasiness and anxiety, accompanying the physiological 'emergency response' including increased muscle tonus.

Ulcer Open sore in the lining of the stomach or duodenum.

Wellbeing General characterisation of the adequacy of one's mental, physical and social functioning.